1509

Open Land
for Urban America

The great question of the seventies is,
shall we surrender to our surroundings,
or shall we make our peace with nature
and begin to make reparations
for the damage we have done to our air,
our land and our water?

President Richard M. Nixon
State of the Union Address
January 22, 1970

Open Land
for Urban America
Acquisition, Safekeeping,
and Use

JOSEPH JAMES SHOMON

an AUDUBON *book*
published in cooperation with the
NATIONAL AUDUBON SOCIETY
by
THE JOHNS HOPKINS PRESS
Baltimore and London

To ERARD A. MATTHIESSEN,
colleague, conservationist, and champion of natural areas
and community nature centers

Contents

Foreword   AT A TIME when such dramatic environmental ills as air and water pollution lay claim to our immediate concern, the disappearance of natural areas and open lands is rather easily overlooked, yet it poses another most serious threat to the quality of the American environment. It may well be more serious than pollution because open land, once developed, is usually gone for good; the loss is, in any case, largely irrevocable in any short span of time, and Americans are estimated to be losing this crucial resource at the rate of some million acres a year.

Occasionally, of course, the loss of open land is of such a nature that in today's climate of opinion it captures the attention of the public. Such an instance was the threat posed by the super-jetport which the Dade County (Florida) Port Authority proposed to build in the Big Cypress Swamp just north of Everglades National Park. There the danger was not merely to the so-called waste land which would have been used for the jetport and ancillary development but to the park itself, the very life of which depends on the quantity and quality of the flow of water from the Big Cypress. The earlier movement to dam the Grand Canyon and the recent attempts to turn the valley of the wild Oklawaha River into a barge canal, as well as the proposed Alaskan pipeline, are comparable examples of the power of public exposure of controversial projects.

Much more frequently, however, the loss or degradation of open land in America proceeds without publicity, usually as a routine manifestation of our "progress." In this way, bit by bit but at a staggering annual rate, the open land in and around our cities is fast disappearing. In the long run, this loss of open land in the very areas where most of our population is concentrated may prove to have more drastic social and even ecological effects than would more spectacular losses in wilder areas.

It is to this problem, and to its possible solutions and alternatives, that *Open Land for Urban America* addresses itself. But this book goes beyond simple advocacy of preservation and protection. It sets out the educational potential of open lands in urban areas, a potential which is very great indeed. Nothing, I think, is more important than for people to come to understand the nature of their life support system. In addition, the psychic value of greenspace—the need of the human spirit to refresh itself through contact with nature, be it a vest-pocket park shielded from city traffic, a woodland or meadow within easy reach of home or work, or simply a countryside unscarred by random development—probably needs no elucidation (although too often it is ignored). But the ecological importance of greenspace is less well recognized. Studies conducted in New York City, for instance, as Dr. Shomon reports, have shown that the large open area of Central Park has a significant role in combating the effects of air pollution by diluting deleterious concentrations of sulfur dioxide. As Roland C. Clement has said, "Today, increasingly, science is documenting the fact that [open space] is a matter of survival for the human race because the planetary ecosystem must continue to function adequately."

Like so many other environmental problems, the disappearance of open space in cities and suburbs has its roots in our tremendous and largely unplanned technological and economic growth and in the population explosion which has accompanied and supported it. Almost before we were aware of what we had lost, much damage had been done. To avert far more damage now, we shall have to move quickly. Dr. Shomon's book points the way.

ELVIS J. STAHR
President
National Audubon Society

Preface THIS BOOK attempts to reflect the urban scene in which most Americans live; it offers ways to make our crowded cities and spreading suburbs more livable and our present and future urban environments more open and natural. The basic premise here is that American life and its setting—which is largely dominated today by the city—can and must be improved.

Haphazard development, wasted resources, tensions, despair, and ugliness have made many cities appalling ghettoes, many suburbs "slurbs." The environment that we have inherited represents a legacy of years of neglect and poor or non-existent planning. We have allowed technology to run rampant and have accepted a life style of instant obsolescence and worship of man-made objects. A change in our view of the land and a new way of life marked by a deeper appreciation of human and natural values is needed if urban areas are to be made more livable, if the suburbs are to be improved, and if satellite cities and even new cities are to be created in suburban areas and in the hinterlands.

We *can* make our urban environments more natural, more appealing, and more beautiful. We *can* preserve open space and wildlife where people live. To make these improvements in our environment, however, new commitments are necessary—new dimensions in thinking, new priorities, and new practical programming. The focus must be on those kinds of planning efforts and land use programs and activities that people really need and are beginning to demand. Nature centers, ecologically oriented parks, outdoor land-for-learning places, greenbelts, specially designed parkways, and unique natural areas all can make the urban and suburban scene more attractive and livable. Case studies are included to show how some cities and urbanizing areas have coped with the land crisis. Some new ways to use urban land and to keep it open are suggested, along with a fresh look at the land itself, its benefits and ecological role in a man-dominated environment.

Many believe that an improved urban environment can make the difference between a drab and disintegrating society and a society which offers dignity, hope, and humanity. For this reason, the "open lands" battle must be engaged and won in the few remaining years of this century.

J. J. S.

Acknowledgments   AMONG THE MANY PEOPLE

who contributed to the preparation of this book, Charles H. Callison and Roland C. Clement, Executive Vice President and Vice President, respectively, of the National Audubon Society, are due special thanks for encouragement and suggestions. The author is indebted for help with parts of the text to Richard Manly, Raymond Kordish, and Jack Allen, all colleagues at the National Audubon Society. Others who helped materially in one way or another are James Fisher, Deputy Chairman of the Countryside Commission, London, William Reilly of Urban America, Inc., Byron L. Ashbaugh, Herbert Johnson, Keith Hay, Dwight Readdie, William Huber, Dr. Merritt B. Shobe, Vern Walker, Russ O. Tocher, Robert F. Holmes, Stanley Ernst, and Marion Clawson.

Government agencies and private organizations which provided material include the U.S. Forest Service; the Bureau of the Census; the Environmental Services Administration; the Bureau of Outdoor Recreation; the New York Department of Parks, Recreation and Cultural Affairs; the New York State Conservation Department; the Wisconsin Conservation Department; the Open Space Institute; the Urban Institute; the Urban Land Institute; the New York Regional Plan Association; the Rouse Company; and Reston, Inc.

The author is grateful to Paul Hess, formerly of the National Audubon Society, for maps and sketches. Photographs not otherwise credited were taken by the author.

Open Land
for Urban America

I | Urban Perspectives and Prospects

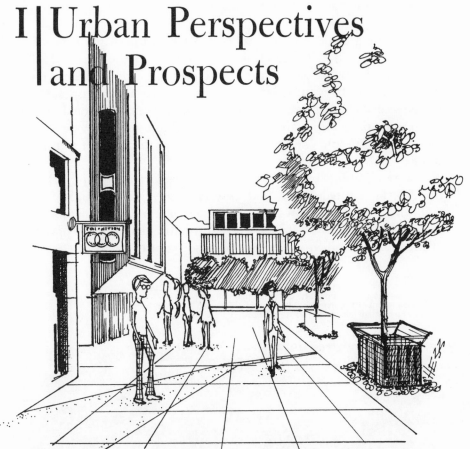

NEWSPAPERS and other news periodicals reflect the fact that our deteriorating environment is of concern to a fast-increasing number of Americans. It has three causes: growth of the population, technological progress linked to increasing levels of consumption, and an appalling lack of environmental planning. Our increasing per capita income and concomitant higher standard of living, increased leisure time, and unfortunate worship of growth, development, speed, and material things, all in an increasing population, put great stress on our environment. For the first time in history we are starting to comprehend the destructive ecological forces that threaten the quantity and quality of the air we breathe and of the land and waters that sustain us. We are starting to show a real concern for—and understanding of—the problems we face in trying to bring these forces under control.

One of the most visible signs of our growing population (which is probably the most fundamental cause of our deteriorating environment) is the growth of cities. Americans began the switch from life in the country to life in the cities and suburbs in the period 1910 to 1920, and the trend still continues. Today more than 75 per cent of the population lives in urban areas. The Census Bureau predicts that by the year 2000 that figure will be over 90 per cent. What will happen when our population approaches 300 million people, which seems likely enough a few years from now, assuming that present trends continue?

The relationship between the American environment and urbanization in the United States, and especially the disappearance of open land and water in urban areas, is the main subject of this book. We shall examine the meaning for American citizens of the disappearance of urban open land, and what can be done about it.

Tapiola, Finland, shown here and on the page opposite, provides a classic example of a desirable new community. Carefully planned and well thought-out new communities, even new towns and cities, can be beautiful, healthful, convenient places to live in. (Photos Tapiola Tourist Bureau.)

The total land area of the United States is approximately 2,266 million acres. This includes all dry land temporarily or partially covered with water, such as marshland, swamps, and river flood plains, streams, sloughs, estuaries, and canals less than 220 yards wide, lakes and reservoirs, and ponds less than forty acres in area.

Three centuries of settlement and population expansion have appreciably changed the American landscape. Cities and roads have been built and expanded at the expense of forest and agricultural land. Today about 2½ per cent of our land area represents cities, roads, and airports. Parks and similar regulated open areas represent about 3½ per cent. Crops cover 20 per cent. Wild land is being used up alarmingly fast. As cities become crowded, there is a spill-out of people to new urbanized corridors, subdivisions, and existing towns and villages. Each year a million acres of land are developed in one way or another.[1] For those who value open areas for esthetic or ecological

[1] Citizens Committee for the Outdoor Recreation Resources Review Commission Report, *Action for Outdoor Recreation for America* (Washington, D.C., n.d. [Apr. 11, 1963], p. 3).

reasons, these developed lands are lost, which is a problem of special concern to city dwellers. In the decade 1950–1960, 97 per cent of the population growth in the U.S. occurred in urban sectors.

According to Ann Louise Strong, a highly respected authority on open lands, "it is expected that the total amount of land in total development for urban purposes will double before 1980. By 1970 our population had become 70 per cent urban, with 97 per cent of the Nation's growth occurring in urban areas. We cannot anticipate all of the long-term and short-term problems that this urban explosion will create; but we do know that unless we act quickly to preserve the best remaining urban open land while it is still available, a large majority of our population will soon lose easy access to the natural environment."[2]

One needs only to make an aerial swing around John F. Kennedy Airport or Chicago or Los Angeles, not to mention a hundred smaller urban areas, to see what urbanization is doing to the American countryside. Meanwhile, in our cities, urban conditions deteriorate. As more and more people flee the city, the tax base of the central core shrinks. Ghettoes arise. The city's heartland decays. The attrition of undeveloped lands and waters in urban America led President John F. Kennedy to point out in his Housing Message to Congress in March, 1961: "Land is the most precious resource of the metropolitan area. The present patterns of haphazard suburban development are contributing to a tragic waste in the use of a vital resource now being consumed at an alarming rate." In 1965 President Lyndon B. Johnson, in his State of the Union Message to Congress, called for "a massive effort to save the countryside and establish—as a green legacy for tomorrow—more large and small parks, more seashores and open spaces than have been created during any period in our history."

The attrition of America's landscape due to urbanization can be seen in the effect on wetlands and parks. Of the original 127 million acres of wetlands in the United States, the Soil Conservation Service estimates that 45 million acres have been destroyed by drainage, filling, levees, and dredging. In New Jersey, for example, nearly 5 per cent of all wetlands were destroyed in just five years, 1954–1959, primarily through filling for residential or industrial purposes.[3]

---

2 *Open Space for Urban America*, Urban Renewal Administration, Department of Housing and Urban Development (Washington, D.C., 1965), p. 1.
3 *Ibid.*, p. 9.

The spiraling human population which underlies many contemporary problems is responsible for almost overwhelming physical strain on some parklands. (Photo H. Armstrong Roberts.)

Urban encroachment onto city parkland in recent years has been severe. In 1969, for example, the director of parks for Atlanta, Georgia, said that his city had lost 60 per cent of its original parkland in the previous thirty years.[4] The threats to parks come in many forms: a highway bypass through Hubbard Park in Meriden, Connecticut, schools in Chicago, an expressway through Overton Park in Memphis, and the possible adverse effects of the new jetport outside Miami on Everglades National Park.

A spiraling human population is the basic cause of the disappearance of urban open land. In the United States the population as of September 1, 1969, was 202,319,000. The explosion of technological know-how is no doubt a prime cause of modern land and water loss and of

[4] Personal communication to the author.

This common type of suburban development is an example of what poor planning, together with spreading urbanization, is doing to much of the American countryside. The ugly conglomerations of houses, acre upon acre, seem pathetic and depressing. (Photo Office of Housing and Urban Development.)

much environmental deterioration.[5] For example, the growing use of automobiles permits people to live in housing developments much further from jobs and shopping facilities than would otherwise be possible; automobiles also permit people to visit, in great numbers, areas that were once considered remote.

The disappearance of urban lands and waters is part of the greater problem of environmental deterioration in the United States. Some writers place the blame squarely on the federal government. Thus, in one popular magazine we find:

[5] Citizens Committee for the Outdoor Recreation Resources Review Commission Report, *Action for Outdoor Recreation for America*, p. 3.

Many of our present environmental difficulties can be attributed to the fact that no single person, agency, bureau or department in the Federal Government has an overall view of what is happening to our land and waters. No one is providing any sense of direction or continuity. Action on a problem comes, if at all, only in response to disaster or after persistent clamor by concerned citizens. Sporadic White House interest in "natural beauty" (referring particularly to the Johnson administration) is so superficial as to be dangerous. The public is lulled into thinking problems are being met. Natural beauty is cosmetics conservation. Instead of applying pancake makeup to the landscape, we should be stopping cancer.[6]

When urban design is dominated by the profit motive, some very sterile and monotonous urban patterns are likely to result. The common agglomeration of box-like houses one after another, row upon row, acre upon acre, subdivision upon subdivision, is pathetic, depressing, and disheartening. If our future environment is to improve, rather than to continue to deteriorate, aesthetics must play a more important role in urban and suburban planning than it has in the recent past. Both Ian McHarg of the University of Pennsylvania and William H. Whyte make a forceful case for designing with nature. McHarg stresses seeing nature first and designing and planning with natural conditions in mind;[7] Whyte argues cluster development in suburbia as one way to save more open space[8] (see also Chapter V, Figs. 6 and 7, for ideas on cluster[9]).

If our central urban areas are to survive, we must contain their size and stop denaturalizing them. As Lewis Mumford says, "We need to provide in them more open space [and] more *living* greenery, more *natural* beauty. Great government schemes of tearing down vast neigh-

[6] "How To Stop the Pillage of America," *Sports Illustrated*, December 11, 1967.

[7] *Design with Nature* (Garden City, N.Y.: Natural History Press, for the American Museum of Natural History, 1969).

[8] William H. Whyte, *Cluster Development* (New York: American Conservation Association, 1964).

[9] The National Association of Home Builders (see Appendix 5 for its address and those of other organizations offering assistance programs) produces an Open Space Kit which discusses clustering developments and ideas in detail. It is available from NAHB each year while the supply lasts. NAHB also has produced a twenty-nine-minute 16 mm. sound movie in color which is distributed free by local branches of Association Films, Inc., whose headquarters is at 600 Madison Avenue, New York, N.Y. 10022. The NAHB, in cooperation with the Urban Land Institute, has produced several technical bulletins dealing with clustering and other aspects of reserving open land in housing developments. For these bulletins, inquiries should be directed to the Urban Land Institute.

"In wildness . . . released from artificial influence, one's sensations change, and with them one's appraisals. The importance of accomplishment gives way to values of awareness."—Charles A. Lindbergh.

borhoods only to erect new sterile, dehumanized structures will not do. We need to give people a sense of ownership, pride of possession, some quiet and openness and extensive and intensive beauty. We need programs of education to change people's values, to recapture a sense of nature appreciation and a new dignity of living."[10]

There is growing recognition that if our cities and suburbs are to be livable and pleasant, some semblance of openness and naturalness, even

[10] "The Challenge of Survival," address to the Bronx Botanical Garden seminar, New York, July 10, 1968.

some measure of wilderness, are essential. As existing big cities are reshaped, vast ghettoes torn down and replaced, and new cities created, government leaders, architects, planners, designers, engineers, and developers should be encouraged to include natural open areas in the new environments they are creating.

Charles A. Lindbergh has observed that if man is to survive on this planet he must combine the knowledge of science with the wisdom found in nature:

> For me, wilderness brings out nature's basic wisdom in relationship to man's. I see the control of populations, the encouragement of coexistence, the superb juxtaposition of unity and diversity to form life's character. Above all I see an ability to choose the better from the worse that has made possible life's progress. In wildness, as in no other environment, elements of body, mind and spirit flux and fuse. Released from artificial influence, one's sensations change, and with them one's appraisals. The importance of accomplishment gives way to values of awareness. The smell of earth, the touch of leaves, sounds of animals calling, myriad qualities interweave to make one not only aware but aware of one's awareness. With stars above, a planet below, and no barrier between or after, intuition reaches out past limits of the mind into a mysticism at which man shies the name of "God." Then I think of listening to an African tribesman describe his people's culture: "We believe God is in everything," he said. "He is in the river, the grasses, the bark of trees, the clouds and mountains. We sing songs to the mountains because God is in them."
>
> The primitive emphasizes factors of survival and the mysteries beyond them. Modern civilization places emphasis on increasing knowledge and the application of technology to man's way of life. The human future depends on our ability to combine the knowledge of science with the wisdom of wildness.[11]

Man needs the beauty of lands and waters, needs to have his heart stirred by wild creatures, wild places, and living greenery. He needs the refreshment and exhilaration of fresh ozone in his nostrils, the clear vision of unspoiled wilderness lands before him. Man's need for a sense of balance and order and for things in their proper places in the environment is one of the strongest reasons for preserving land and water. To preserve some naturalness in our American urban scene demands something more than money and men. It demands an appreciation of intangibles and a feeling of respect and reverence toward the earth and all life that dwells upon it.

[11] Charles A. Lindbergh, *Life Magazine*, December 22, 1967.

II | Urban Open Land and Open Space

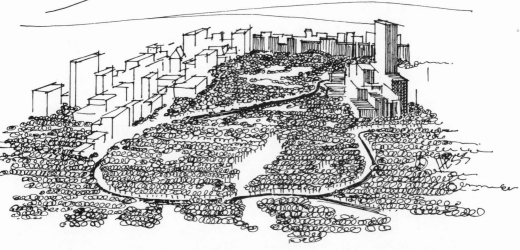

DURING THE CURRENT DECADE concern, both public and private, has been expressed about the disappearance of what planners call "open space." People from the President to the man on the city street are talking about open space and what is happening to it. To some people open space means green space which has been saved in and around our cities—parks, golf courses, wildlife sanctuaries. To others it connotes vacant land not yet committed to development but capable of being built upon. To still others, reservoirs, lakes, rivers, parkways, air space, and just about everything not covered by concrete, steel or asphalt represent open space.

The term may have too negative a connotation. Marion Clawson, for example, states that "open space" stresses the absence of something —an area that does not serve built-up residential, industrial, or other urban land uses.[1] He says that the major aim of many open space proposals is to keep development off—to hold the area open. Some planners may protest this view, but it is true that much of the planning literature does give the impression of keeping development off of open

[1] "A Positive Approach to Open Space Preservation," *Journal of the American Institute of Planners* 28 (1962):124.

land, of preventing the intrusion of buildings, roads, and so on. The term also seems unfortunate to many conservationists, who are not accustomed to viewing woodlands, forests, watersheds, and wildlife habitats as open areas, except in cases like open grasslands, prairies, savannahs, and salt marshes. To them the natural landscape or even the ecological terms "ecosystem" or "greenspace" seem more meaningful.

The terms urban open land, greenspace, greenbelt, parkland, townscape, countryscape all seem somewhat preferable to the negativism of open space and perhaps these more positive terms should be used. Open space as used here means any space in urban America which promotes or has a tendency to enhance the natural environment: any area of land or water or air, whether reserved or unreserved, any green area, any view horizontal or vertical which improves the appearance of the natural scene or the natural environment, can be considered open space. Thus, even another tall building on crowded Park Avenue in New York, if its architect set back its storied sides so that the onlooker gets a better view of the sky as he looks up, can be said to add some desirable open space in the city. But open space and urban open land—land set aside for non-development—are not synonymous.

What kind of land or open space are we talking about? We may consider four kinds of space: reserved land, semireserved land, nonreserved land, and air space.

RESERVED LAND

In considering urban open land the key point is, *what is the function of the land*, or what is the *land use* in question? Here are some examples of reserved lands with specific uses.

PARKLANDS. Parks are areas of land set aside primarily for recreation. Their size in urban areas may vary from tiny sitting parks and miniparks or vest-pocket parks to larger playground parks and sizeable natural tracts of as much as several thousand acres. The administration of such parklands ranges from private, semiprivate, or quasi-public to entirely public ownership and control. Most parks in urban areas in the United States are public parks.

NATURE CENTERS. These are special-use urban land areas, usually undeveloped natural areas—for the most part fifty acres or more in size—that are reserved primarily for outdoor education and training. An urban concept, they have three primary requirements, a land base that is as natural and undeveloped as possible, the facilities and features necessary to accommodate the general public as well as specialized groups (e.g., schoolchildren), and a trained staff to carry out outdoor educational programs.[2] A significant role in shaping our citizens' understanding of our environment could be played by two thousand additional urban nature centers across the country, each with an active education program using the land itself as a basis for learning.

WILDLIFE REFUGES AND SANCTUARIES. These are usually small- to medium-sized land areas (either publicly or privately owned), within cities or in the suburbs, specifically set aside as habitats for wildlife. The terms refuge and sanctuary are interchangeable; the term wildlife is used to denote wild vertebrates, although all non-domesticated members of the animal kingdom can be included. The primary use of wildlife sanctuaries is as habitats or rest areas for wild mammals and birds. In Finland's Tapiola, which is perhaps the best-planned new town in Europe, ducks and other wildlife are fed and take refuge in ponds and pools in the town's center during the hunting season, and many forms stay all year long.

ARBORETUMS. These are largely land areas set aside for the growing and exhibiting of native and exotic trees and other woody plants, usually for scientific purposes. Many colleges and universities have arboretums, as do some city parks and botanical gardens. These preserved land areas can be private or public.

RURAL LIFE CENTERS. These are simply farms or ranches specifically preserved or set aside as educational centers. More and more rural life centers are being established as historical facilities to show urbanites what the small American farm or ranch was like in earlier days. These centers feature educational programs and have on display living examples of the farm scene, including domestic mammals and birds.

OUTDOOR LABORATORIES. Outdoor laboratories are a school concept. They usually involve land adjacent to schools, as well as satellite areas near schools, that can be used by a school or school district to expand the curriculum in outdoor education.[3]

OUTDOOR SCHOOLS, INCLUDING SCHOOL FORESTS. An outdoor school differs from an outdoor laboratory in that it may be a special land area

---

[2] For further information on nature centers, see Joseph J. Shomon, *A Nature Center for Your Community* (New York: National Audubon Society, 1963).

[3] For location and other information, see *Directory of Environmental Education Facilities* (New York: National Audubon Society, 1971).

set aside away from a school to carry out a specific program in outdoor education, either by a school district, school, or private organization. There may or may not be buildings on the land. School forests, on the other hand, are small forest tracts, often presented as gifts to schools, for study purposes and training, as well as for income.

ESTABLISHED NATURAL AREAS. These are small natural lands which have been set aside for their unusual scientific, ecological, or aesthetic value. The Nature Conservancy, a national conservation organization,

Educational farms, such as Aullwood Audubon Farm, provide well-organized educational settings that develop awareness of conservation and farming activities. Here an Aullwood naturalist shows a Shropshire ram to school children. (Photo Aullwood Audubon Farm.)

classifies natural areas in five categories: primeval area, natural area preserve, nature preserve, scenic nature area, and school nature area. These form a spectrum from completely undisturbed situations to developed facilities for education. In all of these some interpretive elements may be present or may be introduced. Non-use is not implied in any of these areas.

RESERVED FLOOD PLAINS. These are areas which have been zoned against development but not against use for wildlife, limited recreation, or education.

There are, of course, other types of reserved lands in the American urban setting, and new types and categories may develop as land use changes and patterns emerge. One thing is certain: no land reservation is absolute. A piece of land is reserved or kept open or green only to the extent that the citizenry, through legal instruments or moral persuasion, is determined to keep it that way.

SEMI-RESERVED AND RESTRICTED LAND

Open land set aside on a less permanent basis than, say, a park can be of several types: a military reservation, an airport, reservoirs, a golf course, a family estate, and so on. As social and physical environmental changes occur, these less permanent reserved areas may be used for urban development or, in some cases, pass into more permanent reserve status. In considering such lands for preservation, one must determine that they fulfill those conditions, legal and otherwise, which allow them to become readily classifiable as *reserved* lands (see Chapter V below). Indeed, this category, these areas, will be the battleground in the fight for open space in the future. It seems imperative, too, that lands in the reserved category not slide back into this middle ground and thus become vulnerable to development. At least half a dozen categories of land can be classed as semi-reserved. They are listed below.

MILITARY RESERVES. The federal government through its military establishment holds title to several million acres of real estate, much of it in urban areas. These lands range from army bases such as camps, forts, and depots to navy, air force, and marine corps installations of varying sizes. Some of these areas are very large, amounting to hundreds of thousands of acres. As military requirements change, many military sites—now in the category of semi-reserved lands—will appear in the market place for disposition. Supporters of urban open land should quickly act to see that such land is preserved as permanent open space, or at least that there is a full public hearing before land use changes or dispositions are made.

AIRPORTS, RAILROADS, HIGHWAYS. While airports may not strike some people as desirable open land, many communities have small airports for private aircraft which are not busy, noisy areas like the large commercial airports. Thus it is quite proper, in an overall view, to value the airport as open space and as semi-preserved land. Moreover, should an airport cease operations, it can either add to the amount of open land available in a community by being converted to a park or wildlife sanctuary or it can be "developed," with a resultant loss of open land. What is true of airports can also be said of unused or abandoned railroad rights-of-way and unused highways and roads. Some rights-of-way already are being used as trails, and there almost certainly will be further railroad and highway abandonment or re-alignment in the future.

RESERVOIRS. Water supply reservoirs are areas of land that clearly fall into the category of semi-preserved areas. Like airports, when put out of use, they can become reserved areas or, as often happens, provide space for development.

GOLF COURSES. The private golf course is more vulnerable to development than, say, the public golf course, which may or may not be part of a public park. In many cases in the past, private golf courses have yielded to one form of development or another. There are ways in which the trend can be reversed and such land given more permanent public status or added to much-needed preserved land in the urbanizing community. The owners or owner of a golf course can sell a development easement to the city or community and thereby keep the area in some form of greenspace (see Appendixes 2–4 for easements).

PARKWAYS, ROADSIDES, RIGHTS-OF-WAY. There is no question that parkways and greenbelts are open land, and that they are valuable and needed. However, many such areas have seen encroachment and obliteration as development pressures, particularly the widening of highways, develop. Thus, these areas, together with miscellaneous roadways and rights-of-way, must be categorized as semi-preserved lands.

UNRESERVED LAND

Lands which are most readily susceptible to encroachment or development are those which are open to sale on the free market. Six major types can be identified.

CITY AND SUBURBAN UNDEVELOPED LOTS. These areas are prime development targets. Still, even under such situations, a change in land use designation can keep some areas open as park or recreation land or a similar special use. Many towns and cities have sizeable acreages in this category. Were they to zone these areas for urban open land, significant amounts of open land could be added to the urban setting. To acquire a mini-park site before development has set in is good business. Once lots are sold on the open real estate market at front or square-foot prices, purchase by the local government is usually out of the question.

SMALL TO LARGE FAMILY ESTATES. Under present American land policy it is difficult for property owners, large or small, in urban areas to keep from being overwhelmed by the taxes that accompany rising real estate values. New formulas and new instruments must be developed to allow such lands, at least those most feasible for this purpose, to remain undeveloped. In later chapters we shall see some devices emerging which lend encouragement here.

HISTORIC SITES. Our nation has seen far too many valuable historic sites deteriorate and then become rubble for the sake of new development. To permit this to happen is folly. Many communities now are beginning to set up controls for the preservation of important historic lands and buildings. In New York City, for example, there is a Landmarks Preservation Commission, a branch of the Parks, Recreation and Cultural Affairs Administration, which has designated many buildings and small areas of land as "historic landmarks" to be permanently preserved. City Hall and its park, Audubon House, and even an old graveyard (Shearith Israel, dating to 1682) are only a few sites so preserved. The National Park Service, of course, preserves historic sites at the national level. Most states and some counties and cities have government agencies charged with historic site preservation. Much more attention to such sites seems to be in the offing.

SCENIC AREAS. When America was largely wild and undeveloped, the idea of setting aside a view or scenic area was almost unheard of. Many planners and conservationists now believe that if America is to preserve the quality of its environment, the urban view must be enhanced by more and more scenic areas. Scenic views, as well as space from which to observe scenic areas, should become a part of so-called ecological planning.

FARM AND RANGE LANDS. Will the typical small farm or ranch disappear from the urban and suburban American scene? There are those who believe the small farm or ranch, even close to the city, can be made to survive, especially if tax incentives are given the small farmer. With agricultural crop prices once again restored to free market levels and with government allowing other incentives to small businesses and curtailing the encouragement of big farming, the small one-family farm could perhaps once again play a vital role in America's agriculture. The big issue here is taxation. For the small farmer to survive near the city his land must be taxed as *farmland* and not as potential development land. Existing trends toward bigger and bigger farm operations, some planners and economists believe, need not continue. There are those in the U.S. Department of Agriculture who believe that the government has the power to reverse the trend.

UNDEVELOPED NATURAL LANDSCAPE. Into this category fall such areas as native forests, shorelines, river bottoms, ridges, mountain tops, marshes, swamps, original prairies, deserts, sagelands, rain forest, and arctic-alpine land. In urban areas when in private hands, without protective devices, these areas are highly vulnerable to development. Ways and means must be found to set them aside as permanent preserves— really, as samples of native America. Some such lands are now being preserved by such organizations as The Nature Conservancy, the National Audubon Society, and various trusts.

AIR SPACE

Preservation of a minimum ratio of horizontal surface space per person is desirable in urban environments, but the preservation of air space between buildings is also desirable. As urban densities increase, air open space looms more and more important. Air space, as one can see from the current clamor over noise pollution, must be given more and more consideration in future planning.

A city, village or urbanizing county seeking to keep its lands open as much as possible must be realistic in its approach to land preservation and safekeeping. It is one thing to acquire or otherwise set aside land. This can and is being done. But it is just as important to safeguard with some degree of permanence what has been preserved, and this is not often being done. Many towns and cities early in their history saw the wisdom of setting aside parks and preserves but eventually lost them completely, or lost great portions of them. They lost them—and these losses are continuing—because they did not construct a strong legal base to safeguard them permanently and did not develop a lively appreciation of their value on the part of the citizenry.

One of the most important aspects of urban open land preservation is the mechanism used to classify land and to approve or disapprove land use changes. Generally this is a municipal planning or zoning board, commission, department, or some such public body. The character and makeup of these bodies is all-important. If they are dominated, as they usually are, by development interests, the community can be in trouble. If the public interest is to be served, it is imperative that these bodies be well balanced and represent a broad spectrum of interest groups so that when land use changes are proposed, every interest group will be heard from. A thoroughly qualified environmental ecologist should be represented on every such board.

A practical classification of open land is no positive assurance that an urban area will have sufficient open space in the future, yet it can point the community or area in the right direction. Both the thinking and classification must be positive: how much reserved parkland does our town or city need today, in 1985, in the year 2000? How much land for learning? How much land in natural features—greenspace, parks, nature centers, wildlife sanctuaries, natural shorelines—does our community need in order to have a healthy environment? These are questions that zoning board members, planners, designers, developers, engineers, administrators, and urban conservationists must keep asking themselves, and they must ponder the answers. When a land use decision is to be made, particularly a change in land use, the all-important question should be how this change will affect the total environment of the community in which we live. These questions are discussed in Chapter IV.

III | Urban Greenspace: Values and Benefits

IT IS BECOMING increasingly clear to many planners and conservationists that if open land is to remain a part of urban America, a higher price tag, not necessarily an economic one, must be placed on it. The importance and value of urban open land, preferably called greenspace or biospace, must be more fully recognized by all who are in a position to effect environmental change. There is a danger that unless this recognition comes soon, in this generation, tomorrow may be too late.

On what grounds can we justify setting aside and keeping land as greenspace in urban America? These are big questions, and no one group or individual knows all the answers, nor has there been enough research to give us all the answers we need. From the scientific and socioeconomic viewpoint, much useful data is missing, and much basic and applied research must yet be done. Between those who are trying to justify urban open land from the standpoint of amenities and the scientists and economists who claim we need more proof of benefits, there is a limited body of knowledge, much of it based upon experience, which says, in effect, that greenspace is vital to man's survival in the urban world. As Roland Clement put it at the Man and Nature in the City symposium held in Washington, D.C., in 1968, "Today, increasingly, science is documenting the fact that [open space] is a matter of survival for the human race because the planetary ecosystem must continue to function adequately."[1] Perhaps the most significant values of greenspace are ecological values and psychic (psychological and aesthetic) benefits. Both are primary values, and proper weight should be given to both.

ECOLOGICAL VALUE

The city is often viewed as an organization rather than as an organism; its mission is to serve man the biological entity, and this is where our trouble begins, the ecologist says. If the urban world is to function properly as a suitable living environment for people, then it is logical to expect that in planning the city, either in reshaping an old one or building a new one, the principles of applied biology and ecology should be taken into consideration.

There are those who would argue that man is by his superior intelligence a highly adaptive animal and can adjust himself to new conditions and create his own environment, that our man-made environment in many ways can be superior to what nature has provided. The counter-argument is that man is not and can never be a totally mechanized creature but must, like our astronauts, still have air to breathe and human lungs to do the breathing; that he still depends upon plants for his existence, because plants manufacture his food and stabilize his atmosphere; that although plants can live without animals, animals (including man) cannot live without plants. Just how much of a plant world we need for optimum livability for man we do not yet know. There is a tendency, for example, to embrace too readily the "lungs of the city" theory in arguing for open space. Although many statements are made about how plants purify the air, this belief, as we shall see later in our discussion of the "greenhouse" effect and air pollution

[1]Roland C. Clement, *Man and Nature in the City,* Bureau of Sport Fisheries and Wildlife, U.S. Department of the Interior, symposium proceedings (Washington, D.C.: U.S. Government Printing Office, 1968), p. 89.

abatement, is only partially accurate. How does modern man interact with the ecosystems of which he is a part?

CARBON AND HYDROLOGICAL CYCLES. We shall review here two natural cycles, carbon and water, which illustrate some important aspects of these questions. Carbon makes up half of the dry weight of plants; it enters the plant as a gas, carbon dioxide (CO_2). Carbon dioxide makes up only 0.003 per cent of the atmosphere, but an excess of 0.05 in the air, as Paul Sears points out, is decidedly bad for animal life, although carbon dioxide is an inevitable by-product of activity in organisms. That the atmosphere remains in balance and suitable for maintaining

FIG. 1. The Carbon Cycle

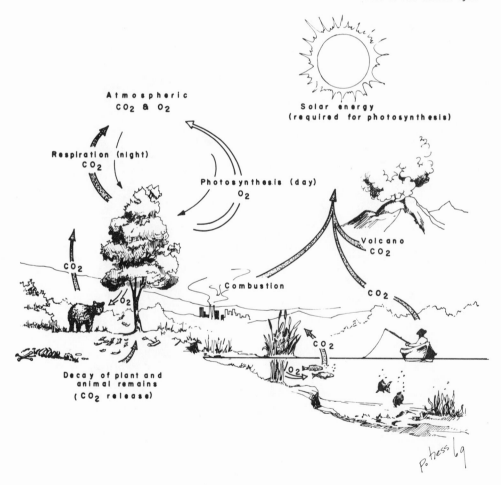

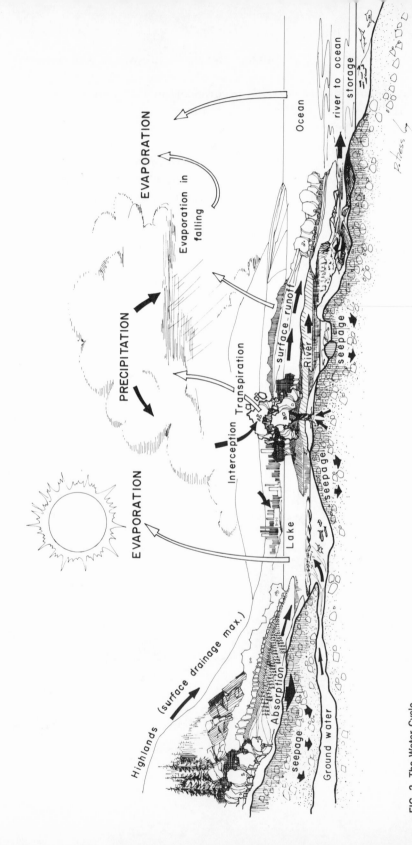

FIG. 2. The Water Cycle

life in both plants and animals is the result of photosynthetic activity of green plants during the daylight period, when they release more oxygen than they need. The only areas where carbon dioxide seems to build up above normal concentrations, Sears says, is in the vicinity of industrial plants and around active volcanoes, and since industry and urbanization go together, the cities are often in trouble.[2] The delicacy of this chemical balance between atmosphere and life is an ecological fact of first importance. By slowing down and regulating the flow of energy from the sun, by displaying a rich variety of biological expression, by cushioning both air and earth in countless ways, plants have come to play a vitally important role in the whole process of life, growth, death, and renewal.

Intricately woven into the carbon cycle is water. Water, the "universal solvent," is essential to all life. Most cells of living things are about 80 per cent water by weight. The bodies of all the more complex animals and plants also have fluids outside the cells which either bathe them or are brought to them through vessels. These liquids, such as blood in animals and sap in plants, are mostly water in which food and other materials needed by the living cells are dissolved. The chemical reactions of life take place in solutions—water solutions. Plants use hydrogen from the water in the process of photosynthesis and release the oxygen from the water into the air.

The water or hydrological cycle, then, is an important system. As water falls upon the earth in the form of rain, hail, or snow, it either sinks into the soil or runs off the surface into brooks, rivers, marshes, swamps, and lakes, from which it may eventually reach the sea (see the figure on p. 24). Soil water may also drain by way of springs into lakes and rivers and then to the sea. However, much water is taken from the soil by the roots of plants. In this soil water are great quantities of dissolved nutrients, such as nitrates and other minerals. The water moves up through the stems into leaves and is evaporated or "transpired" into the atmosphere through small pores, or stomata. The average mature tree, according to the U.S. Forest Service, may transpire as much as fifteen hundred gallons of water in one season. Animals give off smaller amounts of water into the atmosphere. A good deal of water is also evaporated directly from the surface of the land and of bodies of water. The word "evapotranspiration" is often used to describe transpiration

[2] Paul B. Sears, *The Living Landscape* (New York: Basic Books, Inc., 1966), p. 87.

and evaporation. Evapotranspired water circulates in the atmosphere as water vapor until it is precipitated again as rain, snow, or hail.

The carbon cycle and the water cycle together tell us part of our vitally important ecological story and highlight the fact that there is an economy of nature and an ecology of living things, including man, and that the two are inseparable. As Marston Bates has said, "Any attempts

FIG. 3. The Nitrogen Cycle

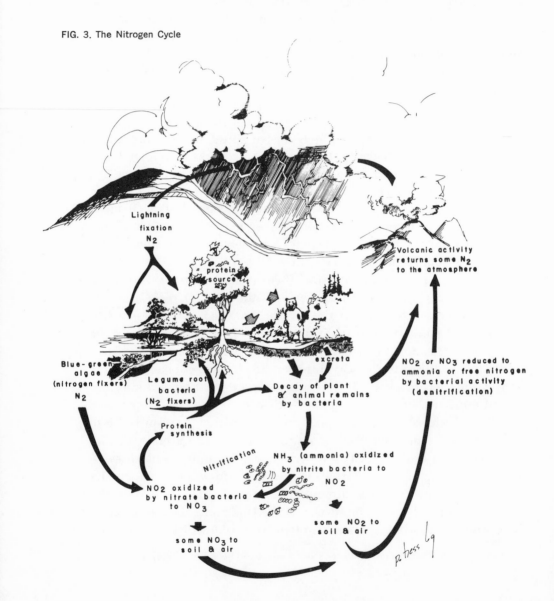

to separate them are more than misleading, they are dangerous. Man's destiny is tied to nature's destiny and the arrogance of the engineering mind does not change this. Man may be a very peculiar animal, but he is still a part of the system of nature."[3]

CONCENTRATIONS OF CARBON DIOXIDE, CARBON MONOXIDE, AND SULPHUR DIOXIDE. The ecological value of urban greenspace cannot be dismissed without further reference to the safe levels of carbon dioxide and other gases, such as carbon monoxide and sulphur dioxide, in the air. Carbon monoxide and sulphur dioxide are both highly poisonous gases and may affect life on earth. The accumulation of carbon dioxide in the air through the combustion of fossil fuels has vast implications for life on earth. Within a comparatively few years man oxidizes (through burning) carbonaceous materials which have accumulated over long periods of geologic time. The result has been an increase in the CO_2 content of the air.[4] If the use of fossil fuels continues to climb, paralleling the growth of economic activity, the carbon dioxide in the atmosphere could increase by more than 50 per cent over its present level by the end of the century. In the long run, atmospheric CO_2 must be in equilibrium with what is contained in the earth's water reservoirs (principally the oceans). While part of the added CO_2 in the atmosphere will be absorbed into the water, it is thought that the process of restoring the CO_2 equilibrium will take thousands of years if carbon dioxide increases as estimated.

What is the significance of all this for man? No one really knows. Atmospheric CO_2 is one of the substances which helps to retain the heat of the sun in the atmosphere and thus may be an important factor in the earth's climate:

> Some scientists believe that measurable increases in temperature have already occurred as a consequence of the CO_2 build-up. Small temperature changes, say an increase of one degree on the average, have profound effects on the world's climate. While few, if any, scientists working on air pollution are willing to forecast the dire effects sometimes foreseen in the popular press, all are concerned. Should effects on climate and other aspects of the human environment turn out to be adverse, we would face a problem of control on a global scale that might require massive efforts to reduce our dependency on fossil fuels. About all one can say at this point is that it is urgently important that we

[3] *The Forest and the Sea* (New York: Random House, 1960), p. 247.
[4] See *Implications of Rising Carbon Dioxide Content of the Atmosphere* (New York: Conservation Foundation, 1963).

observe the situation closely and endeavor to learn more about the role of CO_2 in the determination of climate.[5]

It is interesting to note that some researchers take a different point of view on this matter of climatic change. According to them, it remains an open question whether serious gaseous imbalances are occurring.[6] They give dust and other atmospheric pollutant particles as one reason for the earth's cooling.

And what about the concentration of carbon monoxide (CO, a highly toxic gas, to be distinguished from carbon dioxide, CO_2) in the biosphere? Its concentration has risen, at least in some localities, and many scientists, including ecologists, are concerned. Carbon monoxide was reported to be a minor constituent of the atmosphere in 1949. The average atmospheric concentration is 0.1 parts per million, though urban concentrations are higher.[7] In today's industrialized society production of carbon monoxide is estimated at 210 billion kilograms per year. One of the major considerations, then, is whether, like CO_2, the gas is accumulating in the atmosphere, and this question is in turn related to the average length of time it remains there before being removed by natural processes. One early estimate of carbon monoxide's lifetime in the atmosphere was less than 4 years; another was 2.7 years. Now a study based on radiocarbon dating by Bernard Weinstock of the Ford Motor Company scientific research staff has established a lower limit of 0.1 year. This additional support for the view that carbon monoxide in the atmosphere remains only a short time should help to dispel concern that it is accumulating and that it represents a long-term hazard to human health, Weinstock says (*Science*, October 10, 1969). Whether

---

[5] Orris C. Herfindahl and Allen V. Kneese, *Quality of the Environment: An Economic Approach to Some Problems in Using Land, Water, and Air* (Baltimore: The Johns Hopkins Press, for Resources for the Future, Inc., 1965), p. 33.

[6] There are those who tell us that the earth is not warming up but cooling. Kendrick Frazier, for example, reports ("Earth's Cooling Climate," *Science News* 96 [1969]: 458):

> A central, agreed-upon climatological fact is that the average temperature for the entire earth rose gradually from the 1880's until the early 1940's. At that time a cooling trend suddenly set in which is continuing today.
>
> The worldwide average yearly temperature increased a total of 0.6 degrees C. up to 1940. The cooling since then has cut that increase back by half.
>
> The increments do not seem significant. Yet the fluctuation is believed to indicate a systematic change in the earth's heat budget—the balance of incoming and outgoing energy—during the last century. And the data seem to indicate larger changes in key areas, such as the Arctic, which affect the pattern of atmospheric circulation worldwide.

[7] *Ibid.*, p. 405.

his assertion is correct, however, can only be determined through large-scale research, perhaps world-wide. That carbon monoxide levels in heavily urbanized areas affect human health is already well known.

Another gas which has become a concern in urban areas since air pollution has become a major problem is sulphur dioxide (SO_2). This gas is usually produced by the burning of fuels which contain sulphur impurities. Unlike the pollutant carbon monoxide, which is caused by poor combustion, sulphur dioxide results even with efficient burning. Sulphur dioxide and carbon monoxide have vastly different effects on living organisms. The former attacks susceptible vegetation, is an irritant to respiratory tissue, and will further react and mix with water to become either sulphurous or sulphuric acid. It can erode minerals and corrode metals. Carbon monoxide, on the other hand, is a threat to health alone.[8] It combines with the hemoglobin in the red blood cells so that they cannot carry oxygen in the normal way. When sulphur dioxide concentrations rise, there can be much damage to vegetation, animals, and man. One way to minimize the hazards from SO_2 is to dilute it. Often just moving away from the source of this kind of pollution is a partial answer, and here open land or greenspace is helpful.

Not long ago an interesting study of the SO_2 concentration in New York City was made by testing the air in a line going from the West Side east, across Central Park, to the East Side. The study is reported by Roland C. Clement in a paper entitled "Open Space and the Breath of Life"[9] and is revealing. The study was made by Dr. Ben Davidson of New York University, a meteorologist and student of air pollution in New York City. Clement reports that

> the pollutants emitted by the chimneys of two square miles of residential housing equal the pollutants spewed forth by a large power plant. The power plant's emissions are focused, therefore obvious; the pollution contributed by dense housing is less obvious, and we have not thought of it as of the same magnitude as industry's pollution load. This is of course no excuse for industrial air pollution, but it does illustrate that small pollution sources cannot be multiplied endlessly. So long as we heat our homes with coal and oil, therefore, we will have a pollution problem (other sources of heat have other problems associated with them).

[8] See Stanley Zimering and Kenneth L. Johnson, "The Contaminated Air," *New York Conservationist*, October-November, 1969, p. 12.

[9] Available from Mr. Clement, National Audubon Society.

Dr. Davidson studied the atmospheric concentration of sulphur dioxide (SO_2) in mid-Manhattan, going from the Hudson River to the East River along 79th Street downwind. Remember that this is a single component of the air pollution load, but an important one associated with the burning of coal and oil. The significant feature of this study is the dramatic drop in the SO_2 level created by the presence of Central Park in mid-Manhattan. There are no belching stacks in the park, so being pollution-free itself, it provides an important, perhaps indispensable, dilution of the rest of the community's air pollution load. This is a contribution of every open space, and confirms the earlier conclusions based on good taste and more abstruse evidence, that every community must retain or recreate open space so that it will not suffocate in its

FIG. 4

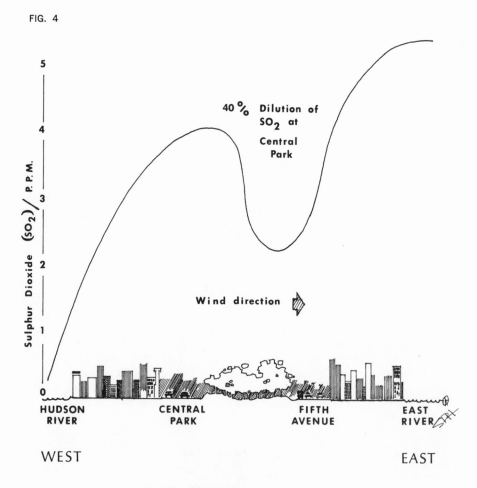

Section Along 79th Street

own wastes. It is a necessary form of spacing out human beings so that they will not completely "foul their nest."

PHYSICAL VALUE

While the biochemical and ecological factors cited may be the most significant benefits attributable to urban greenspace, there are other values that must be noted. The effect of open land on climate, both macroclimates and microclimates, and its role in wind deflection, dust reduction, water control, conservation, noise reduction, and air and water pollution abatement cannot be lightly dismissed. Let us, therefore, examine the claims for these tertiary benefits.

CLIMATE. While forests and other greenery may not have the purifying effects on urban areas that many believe, they do have important effects on climate. To use cover effectively to improve a city, foresters, planners, climatologists, and developers must work together closely. Eric Kuhn makes a good case for planning the city climate. He points out that we must not conclude that greenspace can purify city air and

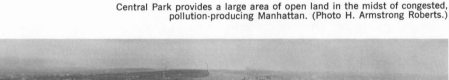

Central Park provides a large area of open land in the midst of congested, pollution-producing Manhattan. (Photo H. Armstrong Roberts.)

function as a cleansing mechanism for excess carbon dioxide.[10] Camillo Sitte showed long ago that a wooded area of three acres can absorb only as much CO_2 as four human beings produce in the course of breathing, cooking, and heating. Kuhn further cites Martin Wagner's finding that to improve the air of Berlin significantly an area of three million acres of trees would be necessary. It was estimated that even Berlin's Tiergarden, which before World War II had half its area in trees, could assimilate no more than $1\frac{1}{2}$ per cent of the CO_2 produced every day in the central district of Berlin.

The removal of large forest areas from the land, as in Iran, Iraq and Greece, may have an effect on climate. Some conservationists believe adverse climatic conditions have been created in those regions. The effect of vegetation on temperature and microclimates is well established: forests cool a city and trees cool city streets, a commonly observed phenomenon and one that anyone equipped with a thermometer can easily investigate and quantify. According to the U.S. Department of Agriculture, "Trees help regulate temperature, humidity and air flow. City streets and skyscrapers store heat during summer days. At dusk when the sun goes down the heat is released [and keeps] temperatures high. Transpiration by trees can counteract some of this heat energy. Along with evaporation from the ground, tree transpiration cools the air, like a gigantic air conditioner."[11] Kuhn cites the tree "ventilating system" used in ancient Babylon. By the careful placement of trees the city was opened to favorable winds sweeping over the city from green Mesopotamia and the Caspian Sea, but closed to the hot winds and desert storms from the west and south. In ancient Greece climatic considerations also played a significant role in street orientation. "In our own part of the world," Kuhn says, "an efficient system would be zones of greenery cutting through all the built up areas."[12] In Russia today the cooling and ventilating effect of wedges of trees around cities is an established and well-accepted planning principle. In Moscow, for example, planned open space is in the shape of a star, with open space radiating out from just beyond the city's center, to provide a cooling effect for central Moscow.

Man's activities have caused quite a few local changes in weather.

[10] "Planning the City's Climate," *Landscape* 8 (1959): 21-23.

[11] *People, Cities and Trees*, U.S. Department of Agriculture, circular, Northeastern Forest Experiment Station, Upper Darby, Pa.

[12] "Planning the City's Climate," p. 23.

For example, four midwestern cities and New York City and Washington, D.C., in the east have had apparently urban-produced increases in annual precipitation and rain days ranging from 5 to 16 per cent and have had 7 to 20 per cent increases in summer thunderstorm days. Thirty miles downwind from the Chicago-Gary industrial area, La Porte, Indiana, has shown far greater increases in precipitation, thunderstorms, and hailfalls—31 to 246 per cent.[13]

DUST REDUCTION. Trees and shrubs are also important in urban areas because they influence the movement of air and filter out dust, airborne ash, and pollen from the atmosphere. Trees also help to abate the problems of water pollution and gaseous air pollution, about which more will be said later. Dust is a major problem in many cities. Apart from affecting health, it is a menace to plants and animals, a nuisance to housewives, and a serious danger to roads, highways, and airports. Each spring the dust storms around Albuquerque, New Mexico, reduce visibility to such a degree that airplanes have difficulty landing and taking off. In the summer of 1968 the author was caught in a severe six-hour dust storm on the Navajo Indian Reservation in northwestern New Mexico, during which many accidents occurred and highway traffic almost came to a standstill.

Greenspace in and around a city reduces dust simply by diffusing the wind. In Leipzig 210 dust particles per cubic centimeter were measured at a spot near where the wind issued from a narrow street, but at the end of an open space two hundred yards long the count was down to 50.[14] Vegetation itself produces little or no dust, except for pollen.

NOISE. Our rapidly swelling urban areas are characterized by a variety of potentially hazardous by-products of science and technology, one of which is noise. The average city is a clanging, buzzing, honking, screeching, whining, shrilling environment. Even small cities like Clearwater, Florida, once quiet and easygoing, are now subjected to the nightmare of whines and screams of police cars, racing ambulances, and fire engines. The roar of "souped up" cars is commonplace in city and countryside. Is this excessive noise really necessary, or as Ian McHarg, the genial but caustic landscape architect and city planner, put it, "Have we all gone mad?" That exposure to excessively high noise levels can impair hearing or cause total deafness is well established. We know less about the effects on health of day-to-day distrac-

13 *Bulletin of the American Meteorological Society*, June, 1969.
14 Kuhn, "Planning the City's Climate," p. 22.

tions of noise—interrupted conversation, disrupted work, and disrupted sleep.[15]

Some people, mostly the young, prefer noise, and many have their ears injured by it. Dr. Walter C. Alvarez, Emeritus Consultant in Medicine to the Mayo Clinic, cites a three-year study of university students by researchers at Germany's Max Planck Institute which showed that a noise level of 70 decibels consistently caused constriction of arteries. Loud noise damages the cells of the cochlea that help transmit sound to the auditory nerve.

The limit of human endurance to prolonged noise without damage to the hearing mechanism is 80 decibels. Ordinary conversation in a quiet setting measures 60 decibels; factory machines can measure 80; a trumpet, 90; a power lawnmower, 96; farm tractors, 97; starting a motorcycle engine or firing a gun, 100; operating textile looms, 106; and the screech of a jet airplane, up to 150.[16] Robert Alex Baron reports that "in New York City, Mayor Lindsay's Task Force on Noise Control recently declared that noise here has reached a 'level intense, continuous and persistent enough to threaten basic community life.' "[17]

Trees and other plants can reduce noise, although it is harder to eliminate than dust is. There is little question about the value of trees, forests, forest strips, shelterbelt plantings, and the like, in decreasing both noise and wind velocity. The U.S. Forest Service says flatly that trees cushion noise, and the U.S. Soil Conservation Service points to numerous examples in the West where cities and towns have been protected from noise and wind to a marked degree by shelterbelts. Moscow, Idaho, and Pullman, Washington, are cities where shelterbelts have worked successfully. More and more state highway departments, like those of Maryland and Virginia, are following a policy of providing strips of trees, shrubs, and vines as dividers for freeways and interstate highways. Multiflora rose is one of the best "cushion" plants for these strips. The U.S. Bureau of Public Roads long has advocated such natural greenery along U.S. highways, a secondary benefit being noise reduction.[18]

We still need to know, however, what kinds of shelterbelts provide

---

[15] See Task Force on Environmental Health and Related Problems, *A Strategy for a Livable Environment*, Report to the Secretary of Health, Education, and Welfare (Washington, D.C.: U.S. Government Printing Office, 1967).

[16] See *Newsday*, November 14, 1969, p. 7A.

[17] "The Invisible Polluter—Noise," *Catalyst*, Spring, 1970, p. 14.

[18] Personal communications and letters to the author.

the best noise protection for different kinds of noises. Are hardwoods superior to conifers in noise reduction, and, if so, in what way and in what combination? What about slope and elevation? Does falling water in combination with trees provide better noise absorption than trees alone? (See the case study in Chapter VIII of Paley Park in New York City, a mini-park that helps absorb noise.) These and other questions must be answered before the planner can make maximum use of these tools.

WATER CONTROL AND CONSERVATION. The efficiency and productivity of greenspace or open land in urban areas in the physical sense are critical factors in determining how much of this kind of space we should have. By preserving these resources, we know that surface water runoff can be reduced, water supplies protected, flood damage prevented or lessened, soil nutrients guarded and underground critical water aquifers safeguarded. The misuse of these natural resources—or the lack of them—has presented us with polluted and silted waters, flooding, water shortages, and decreasing fish and wildlife populations. These facts are well known and need not be documented here. The focus now should be on action programs to set aside open lands and then on sound management of these lands so as to achieve maximum benefit for the most people over the longest period of time. "The dependency of urban settlements on the produce of a well-managed resource system is making the soil conservation agent, the hydrologist, the geologist, and the ecologist essential members of the planning team for the metropolitan area."[19] The concerns of these specialists are not just rural concerns but urban ones as well.

WATER AND AIR POLLUTION ABATEMENT. The water pollution threat in the United States is so extensive, so vast and complex, as to be almost incomprehensible. Damage to water supplies and to plant and animal life runs into millions of dollars annually. A single case in point is a report on fish kills. The Federal Water Pollution Control Administration reports an estimated 15.2 million fish died because of water pollution in 1968, an increase of nearly one-third over 1967 deaths; part of this increase, according to David Dominick of the Administration, may be the result of better reporting, but much of the increase is real. The largest kill in 1968 occurred when chemicals from a petroleum refinery leaked into the Allegheny River and killed 4 million fish. In

[19] William I. Goodman and Eric C. Freund, *Principles and Practice of Urban Planning* (Washington, D.C.: International City Managers' Association, 1968), p. 187.

The air is polluted by waste products of many sorts, including carbon dioxide, carbon monoxide, and sulfur dioxide. There is little that man can do to repair the damage that he has inflicted on the atmosphere, but reducing atmospheric pollution to prevent further damage is usually possible. (Photo H. Armstrong Roberts.)

the same year in Mobile, Alabama, a sewage treatment plant caused the death of 1 million fish. Since June, 1960, 103 million fish have been reported killed in 2,830 pollution incidents.[20]

The damage that water pollution is doing to such critical environments as bays, beaches, general shorelines, and marine estuaries is well known, although an accurate assessment of its total extent annually has never been made. Coupled with these effects, the threat to human life and to the well-being of many other living organisms makes the problem overwhelming. Yet it is being faced, and a beginning has been made in all forms of pollution abatement, including thermal and radioactive pollution. The more pertinent question here, however, is how, in

[20] *Science News* 96 (1969): 377.

urbanizing areas, can open land and water, including plankton-producing waters, reduce pollution? We know now, for example, that polluted air and water harms vegetation, but the question of how the reverse can be true is not so easy to answer. Forest Service researchers have shown that vegetation and soils do filter out impurities from water, slow down moving polluted waters, expose them to the air where they are purified, and so on. Yet much more research needs to be done in the area of environmental ecology.

As for air pollution, this relatively new threat to the living environment is so immense as to stagger the imagination. One expert, Dr. John T. Middleton, estimates that air pollution now costs us about $12 billion a year, or $65 per person, quite apart from its damage to health.[21]

To meet these crises, the experts say, will take a monumental commitment to a program of correction. As Dr. Middleton describes the mission ahead:

> Our goal is to insure that the quality of the air in the Nation's cities and towns does not threaten public health or welfare. Toward this end, it will be necessary to achieve better control in most places of all important types of air pollutants.
>
> There is a substantial body of knowledge indicating which pollutants are particularly injurious to health and welfare. The common ones include sulfur oxides, particulate matter, carbon monoxide, and organic compounds such as photochemical oxidents, nitrogen oxides and fluorides. Our aim is to control the most common and the most injurious air pollutants, whether coming from factories, automobiles, incinerators, electric power plants, or any other source. All major sources must be brought under control or air quality will continue to deteriorate.

The encouraging feature to be noted in all of the air quality talks now going on is the reference to public health and welfare. If the contribution to this goal of open greenspace in urban areas is understood, perhaps the strong argument which I make in this volume will be supported.

ECONOMIC BENEFITS

Whether urban greenspace can be justified solely on the basis of economic values is a moot question. There are those who believe that

---

[21] John T. Middleton, "Air Pollution Threat to Flora and Fauna Doubles Threat to Man," *Conservation Catalyst* 2 (1967): 3.

it cannot and those who say that it can. Among the questions involved are concepts that border on both philosophy and political science, such as whether land, because it is finite, is to be considered a commodity to be sold to the highest bidder in the marketplace, like, say, a hundred-weight of potatoes. Should we not revise our concept of land in America? Most economists and conservationists take the view that urban open land must be argued on the basis of socioeconomic benefits rather than on economics alone. John V. Krutilla makes the observation that "there is a family of problems associated with the natural environment which involves the irreproducibility of unique phenomena of nature . . . that the utility to individuals of direct association with natural environments may be increasing while the supply is not readily subject to enlargement by man . . . and that the real cost of refraining from converting our remaining rare natural environments may not be very great." Our problem, Krutilla points out, is akin to the dynamic programming problem which requires that a present action (which may violate conventional cost-benefit criteria) be compatible with the attainment of a future goal.[22] What Krutilla seems to mean is that some natural environments (and this could involve urban greenspace) have an economic value because of their irreplaceability, which is far greater than has been assumed in the usual cost-benefit ratios. Moreover, the scientific value of certain open spaces (unique natural areas) must also be considered, perhaps in terms of the cost of replacement where replacement is possible.

That open land or greenspace provides economic advantages to a community is well substantiated. Sal J. Prezioso, Executive Vice-President of the National Recreation and Park Association, gives numerous examples of how communities have gained economic advantages by the retention or creation of parklands in their midst—such areas as Cape Cod, Cape Hatteras, the Great Smokies, and other places are all flourishing because of preserved parklands:

> In my travels throughout the country these past few months, I have visited more than 45 states in the Union. My observations permit me to say rather clearly and without fear of contradiction that all dials relative to parkland acquisition and development point to growth and this is subsequent to weighing the economic advantages of acquiring parklands for the community.

[22] *Conservation Reconsidered* (Washington, D.C.: Resources for the Future, Inc., 1967), p. 784; reprinted from the *American Economic Review*, September, 1967.

Public officials throughout the land are saying that it is all too evident that the country must invest more time, money and thought in recreation if we are to attain a suitable environment for ourselves and our posterity.[23]

A strong economic case is made for open space preservation by Charles E. Little in his book, *Challenge of the Land*. Little, who has been Executive Director of the Open Space Institute in New York City, cites case after case of benefits to communities, both positive and negative-positive, by preserving open space. Towns which appear to be of special note are Lexington, Massachusetts, Closter, New Jersey, Lloyd Harbor, New York, and Prescott, Arizona. He closes with the following statement:

> Open space produces municipal income negatively—by costing less to service. It produces it positively by adding value to adjacent properties. It can produce income directly through user fees, or because a desirable open space use is also taxable.
>
> The purpose of acquiring or encouraging the preservation of open space may not be a financial one, but acquisition is nearly always susceptible to financial justification. Indeed, there is so much evidence that open space pays off handsomely for the typical suburban community that the objectors should be saddled with the burden of proof rather than the proponents. They are the ones caught with their tax rolls down.[24]

In discussing economic benefits, the use of taxing power is an important consideration, and governing bodies must explore it thoroughly if greenspace in urban areas is to be preserved in any significant amounts. As Charles Abrams says, "As long as private enterprise is the main instrument in American growth and environmental development, tax levies and tax incentives will be among the dominant factors governing the emergence of the American scene. A series of major studies of federal, state and local tax policies as they affect land development is urgently needed, and I hope it will receive the attention of the city planning schools and the public agencies."[25] Stewart Udall adds: "The time has come for us to use the taxing powers of government as a crea-

---

[23] *Economic Advantages of Parklands to a Community* (Washington, D.C.: National Recreation and Park Association, 1969).

[24] *Challenge of the Land* (New York: Open Space Action Institute, 1968), p. 92.

[25] "Opportunities in Taxation for Achieving Planning Purposes," *Planning 1966* (Chicago, Ill.: American Society of Planning Officials, 1966), p. 258.

tive force for conservation. Why not tax the owners of ugliness, the keepers of eyesores, and the polluters of air and water, instead of penalizing the proprietors of open space who are willing to keep the countryside beautiful?"[26]

SOCIAL BENEFITS

The psychic benefits of urban greenspace are manifold and can be categorized as recreational, educational, and aesthetic. The Nature Center Planning Division of the National Audubon Society and most private education and recreation consultants and planners seem to agree that greenspace, parks, nature preserves, nature centers, outdoor laboratories, etc., provide social benefits because of the function of open land. A park, for example, may provide a place for quiet relaxation or active physical activity such as boating, horseback riding, hiking, and golfing. Educationally, land itself can be a teacher, as a visit to a well-run nature center or nature education camp will quickly indicate. If "the number one goal of education is to learn to understand, appreciate and take care of the natural world in which we live," as the educator S. I. Hayakawa has said, then the value of land in terms of social benefits cannot be minimized. People learn best from firsthand experience: we can learn to appreciate beauty directly from the land and the natural landscape. By providing for relaxation, for the cultivation of a sense of natural beauty and healthy conservation attitudes, and for the release of pent-up energies, open lands can provide valuable social benefits in urban settings.

[26] *The Quiet Crisis* (New York: Holt, Rinehart and Winston, 1963), p. 166.

IV | Planning Considerations

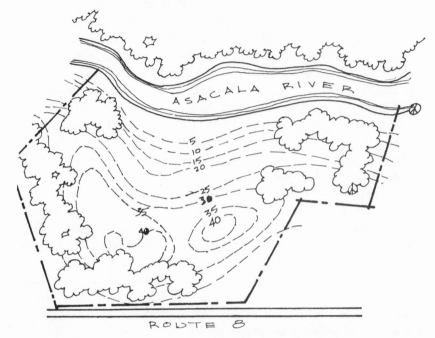

IF AMERICA'S FUTURE is tied to socioeconomic progress and present population trends continue, as seems likely, the reshaping and rebuilding of our existing old cities and the planned development of new ones appears inevitable. What kinds of new physical environments is man to create? A basic resource which must be considered is space. How much land space is needed for the various types of places where man is to live? What problems must be faced in acquiring land, both old and new? Just as important are the location of urban land and its quality.

HOW MUCH OPEN LAND?

How much open land, how much space, do we need in an urban setting? It seems worthwhile to review the usual standards of human density, from villages through urban complexes.

THE VILLAGE. A village is a settlement larger than a hamlet and smaller than a town; it may or may not be incorporated. For our purposes a village will be a settlement with a population ranging from one hundred to twenty-five hundred persons; a settlement less than this is considered a hamlet. Because small villages often are in the habit of swelling in size, especially when located near expanding cities, the amount of open land required should be measured not in terms of the immediate present but in terms of the village's full potential. If, for example, ten acres of open land or parkland per thousand people is used as a standard, then a village of five hundred should not be content to set aside a mere five acres of greenspace. This would border almost on the ridiculous. The minimum might better be twenty-five acres, representing the village's potential growth, plus some additional acreage, not considered essential greenspace, for public buildings. In a similar way, if a village of twenty-five hundred people is destined to become an incorporated town in the near future and its population in time is expected to rise to five thousand, the maximum population level should be used in determining land needs, and fifty acres should be set aside. This viewpoint is based upon the premise that land in undeveloped areas is usually one of the cheapest resources on the market, and a public governing body, as well as a private institution, might better invest in land and hold it while the market value is low than be caught in a bind in later years when money is tight and land values are soaring. Here again, needed permanent greenspace should not be confused with land set aside for urban public buildings.

THE TOWN. A compacted area which is larger than a village and smaller than a city is here considered a town. It should not be equated with the "town" or "township" as the terms are often used in the East, i.e., a rural low-density governmental subdivision. The population of a town ranges from twenty-five hundred to five thousand. As with the village, it is the potential of the town that must be considered when determining open land requirements. A town with a maximum population of five thousand should figure on at least fifty acres of open parkland as its future greenspace requirement. Total land space needs would naturally be higher. Town leaders, therefore, must constantly be aware of the potential growth and maximum size of their communities. If the physical area of a town is fixed and it is not expected to grow into a city, then the standards set may be reasonably adequate; if not, they must be periodically reviewed and any land use changes fully evaluated. It might be worthwhile for towns to have all land use changes involving development (loss of greenspace) reviewed by the next higher land use authority, such as the county. If, for example, the town of Stafford

Springs, Connecticut, were considering a zoning change for a private wooded area within its incorporated limits, and its purchase by a developer was being considered, a higher review would be necessary, in this case, by the Tolland County authority.

THE SMALL CITY. A small city is a settled area whose population ranges from five thousand to seventy-five thousand inhabitants. Any city, but especially those with a higher potential population, should be planning for its future. Park and recreation requirements, as has been pointed out, never represent the total open land needs of a community. The surface of a water reservoir may be called open space, but city fathers may not classify it as recreationally usable open space. As a city grows and its needs become more diversified, its open land areas must be carefully classified and proper allocations made for further expansion.

THE MEDIUM-SIZED CITY. No hard and fast agreement exists among planners as to what constitutes a medium-sized city. Generally, however, a city of from seventy-five thousand to two hundred and fifty thousand inhabitants would fall into this category. How much open land does a city of this size need? We can think in terms of land classification, such as parklands for recreation, both public and private, greenspace, both public and private, and other permanent open space. If the optimum medium-sized city or the new self-contained city is to contain two hundred and fifty to three hundred thousand people, as planned in Sweden,[1] then a full thousand acres of permanent living greenspace should be planned for this urban environment.

THE LARGE CITY. The large city includes all settlements with populations from two hundred and fifty thousand to such a giant, sprawling megalopolis as New York, Chicago, Los Angeles, or Boston. The usual standards for park and open space areas cannot always be applied to large cities. They would not be appropriate for Manhattan Island, for example, where the population is so dense that application of the ordinary standards would mean providing more park area than the total acreage of the island! The New York Regional Plan Association has developed recreation standards and proposed sites for ten new regional parks. It has recommended that 25 per cent of the land in the New York metropolitan area be kept in permanent open space. This total would include twelve acres of county parks per thousand people or 5 per cent of the land of each county, whichever is greater, as well as ten acres of

[1] Chapter VIII below deals with this question of population size and densities at greater length.

local parks per thousand people. (Of course, as indicated above, there are portions of the metropolitan area where population densities preclude realization of these plans.)

The Baltimore, Maryland, Regional Planning Council has proposed the following open space standards:

Facilities	Acres per thousand persons	
	Regional	Local
Public parks and recreation	15	14
Private recreation	2	5
Greenspace	25	17
Total	42	36

This proposed acreage for regional public park facilities is based on a recent study by Marion Clawson of Resources for the Future, Inc., who estimated that, over the next 25 years, there will be an 11- to 12-fold increase in visits to regional recreation facilities in the United States. His prediction is based on a decrease in the work week and work day, in longer and more frequent paid vacations, an increase in spendable income, greater mobility, and, above all, a much larger population.

Rising attendance figures for two State Parks in the Baltimore region substantiate Dr. Clawson's projections. These data, together with surveys in other parts of the country to determine recreational preference, indicated the desirability of the 15-acres-per-1,000-persons standard for regional parks.

The Baltimore local (nonregional) green space standard of 17-acres-per-1,000-persons is a composite of 3 acres per 1,000 persons in Baltimore City plus 25 acres per 1,000 persons in the surrounding five-county area. Green space is defined as land that is "open" in character and used at relatively low intensity. Such use is generally institutional, but also includes nonrecreationally used reservoirs, airports, etc.

Attention also should be drawn to the anticipated flexibility between various categories in the proposed Baltimore standards. The total of 78-acres-per-1,000-persons perhaps is more significant, therefore, than its component parts.

It should also be noted that these proposed standards do not reflect the largest green space uses—namely, agricultural lands, pastures, and forests. Yet the retention of such uses in the more urban areas of the Baltimore region will provide at least part of the open space needs for recreation.[2]

[2] Ann Louise Strong, *Preserving Open Space* (Washington, D.C.: Urban Renewal Administration, Housing and Home Finance Agency, 1963), p. 8.

One mechanism to help keep private land (such as estates or agricultural land) in permanent open space is tax incentives, a device many communities may find effective.

THE URBAN CORRIDOR. Into just what category or classification the urban corridor should fall is something on which planners have yet to agree. Most urban strip developments are simply highly commercialized highways. Many planners view these abominable urban areas as strip-slurbs, a type of ill-planned or unplanned development that no longer should be permitted in this country. Existing strip-slurbs will undoubtedly run their course and, in time, perhaps be transformed into something more in keeping with planned communities.

SUBURBAN AREAS OR SPRAWL. How much open land should an area have that now represents urban sprawl? What are we to do with those suburban areas that simply went wild after World War II, before there was any sign of county or regional planning? Can the engulfment of new areas of the countryside be prevented when development hits them? What about the temporary open land between subdivisions— are these acres truly open? Some answers are emerging. There are some alternatives to haphazard urban sprawl, alternatives which are now beginning to receive serious attention.

One concept already mentioned is cluster development in the suburbs. By clustering housing units of all types together, two desirable ends are achieved, greater densities and more open greenspace. The new cities of Reston, Virginia, near the Dulles International Airport, and Columbia, Maryland, have effectively employed this cluster principle.

There is little doubt today that where good environmental planning exists and there is appreciation for nature, metropolitan suburbia can remain open and livable. One approach is that seen in England, where developments are kept compact, and maximum open space is preserved for recreation, education, and scenic purposes. London has a five- to ten-mile-wide greenbelt surrounding the city, which yields several benefits. It limits the growth of the city, for building regulations are very strict in the greenbelt; it provides unspoiled countryside for the enjoyment of over eight million people; and it provides a degree of biochemical and physical cleansing for air flowing into and out of London. Beyond the London greenbelt the government directs the planning of several new, self-contained towns.[3]

[3] For a fuller discussion of England's approach to new towns and cities, see Chapter VIII.

The Washington, D.C., plan for the year 2000 rejects the greenbelt concept for the already sprawling capital and recommends instead a star-patterned approach to future development. So far, Washington's suburbs represent the most reckless engulfment of open space seen anywhere except around New York and Los Angeles. New towns in the nation's capital area, based on the star pattern, would be self-contained

Reston, Virginia, is an American example of good planning. With the growing awareness of the amenities that new communities can provide, developers in this country can be expected to plan more new housing areas with an eye to ecological, recreational, and aesthetic values. One of the interesting features of Reston is its use of clustering, which permits varied open space near residential areas. (Photo Blue Ridge Aerial Surveys and Reston, Inc.)

communities of from seventy-five to one hundred twenty-five thousand people. Copenhagen has followed this plan but has water on three sides, adding much open space in a three-fingered pattern. In 1985 Baltimore expects to have more than 12 per cent open space in a city whose diversified industry has scattered people throughout its boundaries.

The best chance of improving sprawled suburbs with the least disruption of the homeowner's use of his land lies in greater control over sprawl at the subdivision level. Both the subdivisions themselves and the open land between them needs to be planned and controlled. Newly developed urban areas must tie into planned regional development or risk becoming "slurbs"—perhaps the worst kind of semiurban ghettoing.

LOCATION OF OPEN LAND

The location of open land in the urban setting is highly important. Many large cities in America are suffering from open space problems

A small lake and adjoining public open space in Columbia, Maryland. Such open space for recreational or other purposes is possible (and financially feasible) where "clustering" is used. (Photo The Rouse Company.)

not so much because no open land is available but because it is badly located. The lands were set aside or preserved simply because they were available, not because they were chosen in accordance with a plan. New York City, for example, has many large parks, but, for the most part, they are too far away from the bulk of the population for easy access. More neighborhood parks are needed in high-density areas. Plans are now being made to provide more such neighborhood parks and open

FIG. 5

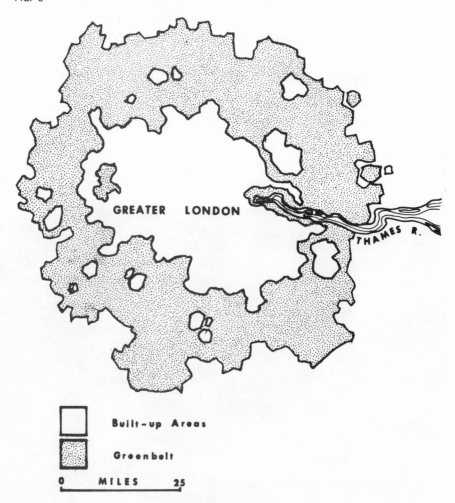

Built-up Areas

Greenbelt

0   MILES   25

lands as redevelopment takes place. One such effort is an ecological park on Welfare Island, planned as a redeveloped satellite city between Manhattan and Queens. The new ecological park—an innovative and unique concept—was proposed by the New York State Commission for State Parks in New York City in a study and plan prepared for it by the National Audubon Society Nature Center Planning Division. The development of this park will be made by the Commission in cooperation with the Urban Development Corporation.[4]

KINDS AND QUALITY OF OPEN LAND

In general, four broad categories of unpreserved land can be seen in most urban regions as well as in the hinterland: agricultural land, forest (managed), pastureland or rangeland, and natural or wild land (wetlands, desert, semi-desert, dune lands, mountain land, etc.)

In trying to determine how much open land a city or community or an urbanizing area needs in the distant future, the category of land in question is important. If a city needs another thousand acres of park space, the character and quality of the land available must be carefully weighed. Steep cliffs, such as riverbank land with excessive slopes, have low usability. An existing park where mugging is common is also not very useful. If only the land of last resort is set aside for parks or nature center sites and quality is not considered, this is plain shortsightedness. The question, then, is not only how much land does a town or community need in urban open space but how much land of varying degrees of quality and usability.

Elizabeth H. Haskell of the Urban Institute makes a strong case when she speaks of clean air, clean water, and useful open spaces as "once 'free goods'" which have become "scarce urban resources. A usably high quality of resource is the scarce commodity, not the quantity itself."[5] As a general rule when land is suitable for one use, such as development, it is also suitable for a number of other competing uses. Parks and nature centers should not be put together from "leftovers" but from land of good quality with elements of diversity. Physical factors which should be carefully evaluated when acquiring open land as permanent reserves are slope or gradient, geomorphology, soil,

---

[4] Further information on this park and plan may be obtained from the State Park Commission for the City of New York, 380 Madison Avenue, New York, New York 10017.

[5] "Quality of the Urban Environment—the Federal Role" (Washington, D.C.: Urban Institute, 1970), p. ii (quoted by permission).

drainage, exposure, elevation, location, and vulnerability to misuse or encroachment. Perhaps just as important as these, if not more important, are ecological factors.

ECOLOGICAL CONSIDERATIONS

Our recent adventures in outer space have not disproved the assumption that the green earth is still the only planet in our solar system which supports what we would call life. The living portion of the earth, the so-called biosphere, is a thin and fragile envelope, but man has become a powerful force on earth and is beginning to alter this fragile, life-supporting environment. It seems imperative, therefore, that the ecological values of land be fully recognized in planning. It is not enough merely to set aside a given area. The ecological values of the land chosen for preservation must be considered; these are variety of land form, presence of water, and diversity of plant cover and wildlife. Where there are options, they should take precedence over such things as building sites, parking lots, highways, thruways, etc. The planners of the East River Drive and the West Side Drive in New York City did not take such values into full consideration. Both riverfronts could have become park corridors for walking, or biking, or just sitting—looking at the water. Instead, expressways were constructed along the riverbanks whose noise, fumes, and general confusion overwhelms any recreational values that might exist. These waterfronts could have become ecologically and aesthetically valuable areas, but "practical" considerations ruled them out. Similarly, Battery Park, at the southern tip of the island, could have been planned and, to some degree, preserved as a naturalistic park. Instead, it is a formal, somewhat lifeless area of much concrete, row upon row of identical trees (all sycamores, all the same size), and much iron and asphalt. So far as park values for its residents are concerned, almost all of the periphery of Manhattan has been "sterilized." In planning our urban environments we should not repeat such mistakes. Natural values and beauty must be given equal weight with "practical" requirements.

IMMEDIATE AND LONG-RANGE HUMAN NEEDS

Environmental planning demands perspective. The first is that of the immediate future. What kind of land, and how much of it, does our city need in, say, the next ten years? Second, what will the needs of our city be by the year 2000 and beyond? Should we be considering long-term financing? What about floating bonds to ensure that the land and its natural beauty will be there when we need it? These are questions that every public body charged with urban land control should be asking. In Florida, outside of Clearwater, a new junior college has a parking lot that occupies a greater area than the main building. Can we afford the luxury of devoting this kind of space to automobiles?

The East River Drive in New York City is a waterfront highway where noise, traffic, and fumes predominate. Although Manhattan Island offers the possibility of miles of waterfront parks, most of the waterfront is occupied by expressways like this. (Photo *New York Times.*)

PROBLEMS OF LAND ACQUISITION

The acquisition of open land in urbanizing America is not an easy proposition to face—anywhere. Land is not an expandable resource; its quantity remains fixed, and there is strong competition for it.

AVAILABILITY. Availability is one of the several keys to preservation. Unless some land is available, or potentially available, for use as permanent open land space, not much can be done. In many cases land is available for certain uses but not for others. Several city blocks in a ghetto area could just as well be used for a park as for housing or commercial development. The point at issue is the best and most essential use of this land. Were the developer strongly motivated toward open land preservation, he could show options for its use. If the city fathers and city residents have been impressed with the fact that open land or greenspace is needed and wanted in the central city, the chances are better that some leveled areas will be devoted to open land projects.[6]

Outside of Cincinnati, Ohio, Stanley Rowe, a retired banker, saw the need of some "lands for learning." He formed a private nature center association and bought the Kripendorf estate, 190 acres containing a fine house and a large woods planted with daffodils. Each spring the estate was a mecca for urban Cincinnatians. It was surrounded by farms and emerging suburbia. Mr. Rowe bought up farmland quietly, along with some houses and lots bordering the nature center, and he now has approximately a thousand acres of green in a fast-urbanizing area. The Cincinnati Nature Center is a thriving and enriching place, and the citizenry seems more nature-minded than ever. Mr. Rowe puts his finger on the reason for the influence of this fine nature center: not only do close ties exist with the city and county but also with the school districts and the University of Cincinnati.

LEGAL BOTTLENECKS. Often land is not readily available for open land preservation because of legal bottlenecks that may exist. These vary from problems of ownership and restrictions on land use to such things as restrictive legal clauses prohibiting sale to certain groups and suits pending in the courts. Whatever the legal problems, they must be solved or at least worked out to some satisfaction before acquisition can proceed.

---

[6] Recently in New York City a four-block area in the ghetto, the site of an old brewery, was demolished. What is being built in an already crowded slum area is another housing development, with higher densities than before. Had the private developer some incentive to do so, this area could have been made into a much-needed mini-park.

COSTS. Costs are the chief single factor controlling the availability of land in any urban space program. Gone are the days when land was cheap—when any organization, agency, or individual could buy all that was wanted. In the span of fifty years, land costs in and around cities have risen astronomically and, unless conditions change, which seem unlikely, will continue to rise. If urban natural landscapes are to exist in the future in America, it seems apparent that the current market value cannot remain the sole criterion for the acquisition, use, and control of land.

OWNERSHIP AND CONTROL. Who owns what land and what degree of control does the owner exercise over it? These matters constantly preoccupy those who wish to acquire land. Control over land is a relative matter, largely associated with who owns it. Degrees of control range from high to very low or none, and their relation to ownership may be pictured as follows: *high* degree of control, government agencies (e.g., a military reservation); *moderate* degree of control, public institutions (e.g., a college or university property[7]), semipublic institutions, industry, wealthy families; *low* degree of control, private farmers, commercial owners in an area of descending property values, developers (e.g., ill-planned private housing).

ROLE OF GOVERNMENT

The role of government in land acquisition for natural landscape in urban areas is a primary one. Both the federal government and the states are now recognizing their responsibilities and are beginning to initiate land purchase programs on a wide scale. The federal government has four main kinds of acquisition programs. Two are programs of outright assistance to states and local communities; others are programs directly run by federal government agencies. The Open Space program of the Department of Housing and Urban Development assists state and local governments in urban open land acquisition. The Department of the Interior Bureau of Outdoor Recreation has a similar grant program for land acquisition, mostly for parks and recreation.[8] The National Park Service frequently acquires and manages historic or recreational lands in or near cities, and the Fish and Wildlife Service has wildlife refuges in urban areas, like New Jersey's Great Swamp.

[7] Yale University owns several thousand acres of forest land in Windham County, Connecticut, some ninety miles from its New Haven campus; control is moderate here.

[8] For full particulars the reader can write to these departments in Washington, D.C.

There are other federal agencies, like the Forest Service, Soil Conservation Service, and Bureau of Land Management, which are interested in the urban problem.

What is lacking in America, however, is a strong land policy and some central coordination of land use. A national planning authority with powers to buy or otherwise acquire future public urban land is what is called for. Such an authority then could commence a program of nationwide planning. It should have a counterpart in each state so that much of the planning within states could be under state control.

The problems of urban land use are complicated in America by our traditional view of land ownership. We have a tradition that an owner can do what he pleases with his land. But land is a finite and vital resource, and we may have to modify our traditional concepts of land ownership. Particularly in urban areas, the public (represented by a governmental or a quasi-governmental body) should have a greater voice than it usually has today in regulating land use.

Some guidelines for America may be found in England, with whom we share so many traditions and where land use regulation has a long history. There planning is much more centrally controlled than in the United States. Private investors are brought into the picture by a sort of marriage of government and private enterprise. Planning is a governmental responsibility, but private enterprise is responsible for management and for carrying out the plan. Land is no longer merely a commodity; it becomes a national investment in which the public has a vital interest. Speculation, therefore, is very much removed from the land exchange business in England. When land exchange (change of temporary ownership) takes place, the public rather than the individual is likely to benefit. In addition to a greater voice for the public in land use, we need an inventory of what we have, particularly an ecological inventory of our remaining open land. This is important to help us determine how much and what kind of land we need to support our population. Only a national inventory of our environmental assets can give us the kind of information we need today to help us make wise land-use decisions.

The problems of urban areas do not end at the borders of the city. They are more likely to be regional in scope, and to be influenced by so many factors that they cannot be effectively solved piecemeal. A *systems approach*, one that considers the entire complex of interrelated problems, is needed. Other countries are well ahead of the United

States in devising and using systems approaches to planning. One example is to be seen in Paris' master plan. In more than one way, Paris is the heart of France. Her master plan is part of a vast regional and national coordinated strategy that is already underway. It includes a design for suburban cities connected to Paris by high-speed rail lines and expressways and complete systems planning for traffic, service needs, parks and open space, and waste disposal. In Sweden, which provides another very successful example, planning is highly developed. Sweden has no slums, urban sprawl is unknown, and poverty is absent. Planning here is focused more on municipalities than on larger regions, but the municipalities have powerful expropriation rights, and the system has produced good results. Stockholm, for example, is a stunning, beautiful city of 1.3 million people, one of the finest capital cities in the world. Architects, planners, and city officials from all over the globe come there to observe Sweden's environmental planning and its systems approach to development.

STATE GOVERNMENT AGENCIES. The fifty states now do have assistance programs through the various federal programs mentioned. The Bureau of Outdoor Recreation program has had enormous salutary effects on urban park space and general outdoor recreation programs; to a lesser extent this is also true of the Open Space program of HUD. These programs, however, need to be strengthened at the state level: perhaps outright grants should be given to states so that more money is channelled into local land acquisitions programs. Were the country to have a national planning authority and the states comparable statewide planning authorities, much better planning results could be achieved. For example, why should not the federal and the state governments begin acquiring land now for future new cities? A matching fund program for "land banks" might well be worth considering.

LOCAL GOVERNMENT. The role of local government in land acquisition (of public land areas) needs to be greatly strengthened in the future, but it can only become stronger if there is better funding from the states and federal government, which might be possible under the proposals mentioned.

THE PRIVATE SECTOR. What about the private sector? Here again, centralized nationwide and statewide planning could do much. The private sector could best provide the local development, management, and safekeeping of those areas planned by the government, which in essence is very much what we see in England, Sweden, Finland, and

France. In Finland, for example, a whole new town (Tapiola) was built by private enterprise, but the planning for it was mostly done by governmental planning authorities.

COMMUNITY SUPPORT

The acquisition of open land in a community must have community support. Whether government bodies or private groups organize to take the initiative, a favorable climate toward land acquisition must prevail or development soon will outrun land preservation. How to gain public support for land acquisition and worthwhile open land projects and activities will be covered in more detail in Chapter VI.

OLD AND NEW APPROACHES TO ACQUISITION

Traditional methods of land acquisition include gift or donation, land exchange, and condemnation by government order or the courts. In addition, there are several new approaches to the preservation of open land, including purchase of land and leasing back (lease-back), immediate purchase and resale with restrictions, suburban development districts, conservation easements, nature easements, and aesthetic easements.

Land for open space uses in accordance with government plans can be purchased by federal, state, or local governments and leased to private persons. Some open space objectives are realized thereby, but a possible disadvantage in this arrangement is the government's assumption of permanent landlordship, with management responsibilities. The removal of land from the tax rolls is also a drawback. Government purchase of land and subsequent resale in accordance with a specific development plan that includes provision for permanent open space is a similar approach which does not put government in the role of a landlord.

Charles Abrams of the Harvard-M.I.T. Joint Center for Urban Studies and Marion Clawson of Resources for the Future have each proposed a variant to purchase and resale. Abrams proposes that governments buy large tracts of land in advance of development, plan subdivisions with inclusion of adequate open space, then sell the land to developers for building sites in accord with the plans. This is an adaptation of urban renewal methods to undeveloped suburban land. Clawson recommends creation of new units of government, called suburban development districts, to plan and develop suburban land within the districts. When development is complete, the district would be disbanded. He suggests that counties or states could preserve open space outside the districts by permitting development only within district boundaries. The Abrams and Clawson proposals would require public support for more complete government control of land development. If these proposals were adopted and result in limiting development to government-owned districts, some form of compensation probably would be necessary, for owners of such land could claim that forbidding them to sell for development would be taking their land without just compensation.

CONSERVATION EASEMENTS. A conservation easement permits the owner of the land to place a restriction upon the land under easement. An easement is a right that somebody buys. For example, if the State of New York wants public fishing permitted on a mile of private brook owned by Mr. Jones and owns land on both sides of Jones's property, it can buy a fishing easement from Jones for twenty-five or fifty or ninty-nine years or permanently. Farmer Jones can continue to farm his land, but he must now permit public fishing in his brook. Such an easement is permanent and transfers to subsequent owners of the land.

The purpose of a conservation easement is to assure the permanent preservation of land in its natural state or in whatever degree of naturalness the land possesses at the time the easement is granted. It can be very rigid or quite flexible. It can cover an entire property or only designated parts. It can forbid change of any kind, or it can contain permissive clauses covering various situations that might arise. A conservation easement might be donated by a landowner or sold to the government for a consideration. If donated, an income tax deduction would be allowable. Such easements offer a special opportunity for the landowner to assure the preservation of parts or all of his unspoiled lands and yet to enjoy their ownership and occupancy and to be able to transfer this ownership to his heirs or others, subject to the terms of the easement.[9]

Open space easements need not grant public use in order to serve a public purpose. They can be used to protect a water supply, wet areas valuable for flood control, a wildlife habitat, or to preserve the rural aspect of a community for purely aesthetic reasons. It would protect a bridle path or woods trail better than any other device.

[9] See *The American Eagle*, No. 42 (1968); see also Appendix 4 for samples of easements now in use.

William H. Whyte, author and specialist on open space problems, advocates acquisition of conservation easements, often called development rights, to shape development and to preserve natural resources. Conservation easements would specify and limit the changes to buildings, landscape, and land uses which property owners may make and might also permit limited public use of the land. The device permits the government to pay less than the full fee cost of the land and permits the land to remain in private ownership, subject to some taxation. It imposes no maintenance costs on the community.

Its disadvantages are that the easement rights must be described with great specificity to meet legal requirements; a severe financial strain may be imposed on the acquiring government by simultaneous acquisition of either the fee or the easements, simultaneous acquisition being necessary to protect all of the land in a proposed area against subsequent conflicting or harmful development; and focus on the land's development potential could lead to an overstatement of this potential by each owner, thus inflating the cost of easements. For these reasons, some fear that the cost of conservation easements in urban areas may often approach the fee cost of the land. Whyte strongly urges that conservation easements be used in combination with other controls, ranging from fee acquisition to zoning, so that each serves where most appropriate and most effective.

Easements can be both public and private, depending on who wants them. A private utility, for example, often buys an easement from a property owner to put a power line across his land. Since 1959, several states have enacted legislation permitting government acquisition of conservation easements and other less-than-fee rights in land for open space preservation purposes. In New Jersey, the state and its municipalities may acquire rights in land by condemnation. Minnesota permits condemnation proceedings by a county, and Oregon authorizes the use of these powers by a specified state agency. Lack of the power of condemnation severely impairs the ability of governments to preserve large, contiguous tracts of open space.

There has been little experience with conservation easements in urban areas, but the scenic easements along the Great River (Mississippi) Road in Trempealeau and La Cross counties acquired by the Wisconsin Highway Commission provide a basis for comparison of easement and fee costs in rural areas. Between 1952 and 1961 scenic easements were obtained along approximately fifty-five miles of this road. Condemnation was necessary for 24 per cent of the parcels acquired. A comparison between easement and right-of-way costs since 1957 on Great River Road points up the relative economy of scenic easements, at least in rural areas. The total right-of-way condemnation cost was $1,151.69 per acre. Scenic easements along the right-of-way were acquired at a cost of only $35.66 per acre.

PRIVATE ACTION. Acquisition of open space is not a goal for governments only; many civic groups, including watershed associations, park foundations, and wildlife and nature conservationists, have had marked success in preserving open space for one or a variety of purposes. The Trustees of Reservations in Massachusetts, the Natural Lands Trust in Philadelphia, and the St. Louis Open Space Council are private agencies active in obtaining and maintaining land for scientific study, conservation, and the preservation of open space. Frequently people are willing to donate land or interests in land to an organization whose goals parallel their own.

A private group may have funds available for prompt acquisition of an area threatened with loss of its open space character. The group later may turn over this land to a public body for maintenance and public use. A recent outstanding example of such action was the purchase of two thousand acres of the Great Swamp in Morris County, New Jersey, by the Great Swamp Committee of the North American Wildlife Foundation and the later deeding of this tract to the Department of the Interior for administration on behalf of the public.

GIFTS OF LAND. Gifts of land from private citizens are responsible for over 50 per cent of new park lands. This fact is surprising when it is noted that the donations occurred, and continue to occur, during a time of rapidly disappearing open land and rapidly rising land values. Government land acquisition for open space uses has been unable to keep up with the demands of our expanding population and has been quick enough to save natural areas from destruction as a consequence of rapid economic growth. Participation by a greater segment of private landowners is needed to help maintain a healthy balance between land for open space and land for other uses in our communities.

Over and above pure altruism, there are a number of concrete advantages to donating land. If we are to reach the generally accepted level of 25 per cent of the area of each community in open space, rather than maintain the present level of less than 5 per cent, we need to make known the sizeable tax deductions, public appreciation and commemoration, and other satisfactions accruing to land donors.

Charitable Tax Deductions. Federal income tax law allows sizeable tax deductions to donors of land to public agencies and approved charitable organizations. Up to 20 per cent of the donor's adjusted gross income may be deducted for donations to approved organizations in general, while up to 30 per cent may be deducted for donations to government agencies and to charitable organizations meeting certain additional qualifications.[10] The deduction amounts to the fair market value of the property at the time of the donation.

At least two conditions apply if the value of the donation exceeds the amount of the maximum legal deduction: the excess over the amount of the deduction may be carried forward over the following five years, or if the donor wishes, the gift may be spread over a longer period of years by deeding an undivided fractional interest in any year. The amount of land donated is not limited by tax law, and the most advantageous arrangement to the donor should be investigated and applied.

Other Tax Advantages. Land which has increased in value since it was acquired will, when sold, fall under the capital gains provision of the federal tax laws. When donated to approved agencies or charities, however, such land is exempt from capital gains tax. This tax break is in addition to a charitable deduction on the entire fair market value of the property, provided this falls within the maximum limits as previously discussed. If the property is sold at the original cost or for some value less than fair market price, the difference between the two can be claimed as a charitable deduction. Payment in excess of cost is liable to capital gains tax.

Reserved Life Estate. Reserved life estate simply means that the donor or his family may continue using the property for life. The charitable tax deduction provisions apply to the present value of the donated interest as determined by actuarial tables used by the Internal Revenue Service.[11] It is also possible to donate a combination of interests, such as a scenic or conservation easement, in addition to the reserved life estate. The value of the easements for life plus the present value of the donated interest represent the available deduction.

10 Internal Revenue Code and Regulations, I.R.C. 170(b)(1).
11 Internal Revenue Code and Regulations, Reg. 25.2512-5.

Gifts and Wills. Making a gift of land to a charitable organization during the donor's lifetime has a decided tax advantage over leaving the property by will. Although in neither case does the estate pay an inheritance or estate tax, the former has the added advantage of enabling the owner to claim a charitable deduction in the year of the donation and in succeeding years if necessary. A gift of land made during the donor's lifetime also simplifies settlement of the estate and reduces probate costs. In addition, the donor maintains control over the details of the gift and sees it become a reality according to his wishes.

OTHER DONATIONS

There are many ways of making a contribution to help save open space for public use other than gifts of land. Gifts of stocks, developed real estate, cash, or other property will be accepted and administered by many government and private agencies established for this purpose. Such donations can be designated as a memorial in accordance with the donor's wishes.

V | Safeguarding Urban Open Land

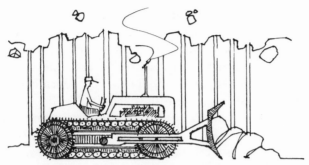

BECAUSE URBAN LAND is limited and fiercely competed for in the market, a vital question is how do you keep urban land open or undeveloped once you have it? Every park director knows, for example, that it is one thing to acquire open space in the path of development but quite another to keep it open. The pressures on undeveloped land in urban areas are enormous, persistent and mounting. Those who oversee critical greenspace are constantly threatened by one form of encroachment or another and must be stouthearted if such lands are to be preserved.

Threats to open land come from government agencies, industry or business, and groups or individuals. It was the State Highway Department, in concert with the city officials in an unpublicized action, that allowed a bypass to be cut through the heart of Hubbard Park in Meriden, Connecticut. The same was true in Overton Park, in downtown Memphis, Tennessee, where an expressway is planned through a superb wooded park. In New York City the Sanitation Department, with official sanction, turned twenty-seven acres of Pelham Bay Park into a garbage dump. In the federal wildlife refuge in New Jersey's Great Swamp, public and private dumping of garbage and litter occurs. In Rye, New York, several landowners have extended their backyards right onto the property of the Rye Nature Center.

Urban open land most frequently is threatened by freeways or other roads, housing development, hospitals, armories, schools, museums, and memorials. Highways have been one of the most frequent invaders. Louisville, Kentucky, will lose one park and parts of two others for highways, and Wilmington, Delaware will gain a new expressway at the expense of forty acres of parkland. In Toledo, Ohio, parklands have been turned over to a naval armory, a YMCA building, a police pistol range, a private yacht club, a sewage disposal plant, and a factory parking lot.

Where it is found necessary to build essential facilities on reserved open land, such as parkland, there should be a requirement that lands lost for park or other open land purposes be replaced with other lands of equivalent size, usability, and quality. Several kinds of safeguards are being used to keep open land open. The consideration here is mainly how to preserve land once it is acquired. The question of acquiring land with safeguards is a subject treated elsewhere in this book. Under legal safeguards come such devices as zoning, cluster development, subdivision controls, official mapping, and citizen action through the courts.

ZONING

Zoning is normally a municipal function and is protective only to a degree. Unfortunately, zoning laws can be changed and are particularly vulnerable to pressure groups who have special interests. An important point here is that zoning laws or ordinances should be based on long-range needs and objectives and that they should not be subject to change by pressure groups such as developers without a full public hearing. Zoning ordinances should never be changed until all public and private interests have been heard from and after all who approve changes (which means land use change) are made fully cognizant of what the change will mean in terms of possible effects on the total environment.

In the United States zoning is the major tool in land use control. Although zoning cannot always withstand the pressures for development and does not necessarily produce land for public open land needs, as purchase does, it can help preserve existing land features. According to the Outdoor Recreation Resources Review Commission report:

> Agricultural zoning, for instance, has been a means of preserving excellent agricultural land and preventing its loss to urban development in Santa Clara County, California. Flood-plain zoning can protect valleys from unsafe developments and preserve natural areas. Even within built-up areas, zoning regulations can provide for more outdoor recrea-

tion if greater flexibility in setback requirements permits the clustering of dwelling units, with increased open space in between the clusters.

Subdivision regulations, another form of zoning, can expand opportunities for a community by requiring developers to reserve a certain percent of subdivision land for recreation purposes or, in lieu of land contribution, to pay a fee to a local park fund.[1]

CLUSTER DEVELOPMENT

Cluster development is a form of zoning and is, in effect, a change in the pattern of development itself. Until recently, as the ORRRC report points out,

> communities thought big lot sizes would guarantee open space, but, in the typical subdivision, this hope proved to be an illusion; big enough to have to mow, too small to use, and a perfect amplifier of sound. Instead of forcing subdividers to chew up all of an area with rigid lot sizes, some communities have suggested that they group the houses in a tighter, more cohesive pattern [see the illustrations of two types of cluster patterns below]. This saves money for the developer, for he does not have to provide as much asphalt and service facilities. It may pay him to leave anywhere from 40 to 60 percent of the land open and, as part of the bargain, this is deeded for common use of the residents. Instead of a miscellany of back lots, there can be bridle paths, playgrounds, wooded areas and—that most desirable of community assets— a stream, flowing in the open and not buried in a concrete culvert.
>
> The potential of a series of open spaces is great. The open space of each cluster development can be planned so that it can connect with others; by wise siting of publicly purchased land for parks and schools, there can be a unified network of open space in which each element contributes to the others.[2]

SUBDIVISION CONTROL ORDINANCES

While used to a lesser extent than zoning, subdivision controls are used to some degree to maintain urban open land. By regulating the type of subdivision to be built and the requirements for sewage and water, municipal ordinances sometimes include open space provisions.[3]

---

[1] *Outdoor Recreation for America*, a Report to the President and to the Congress by the Outdoor Recreation Resources Review Commission (Washington, D.C.: U.S. Government Printing Office, 1962), p. 150.

[2] *Ibid.*

[3] For fuller treatment of subdivision controls, see *Open Space for Urban America* (Washington, D.C.: Urban Renewal Administration, Department of Housing and Urban Development, 1965), pp. 39-40.

FIG. 6. In the typical subdivision, the hope that large individual lots would guarantee open space has proved to be an illusion.

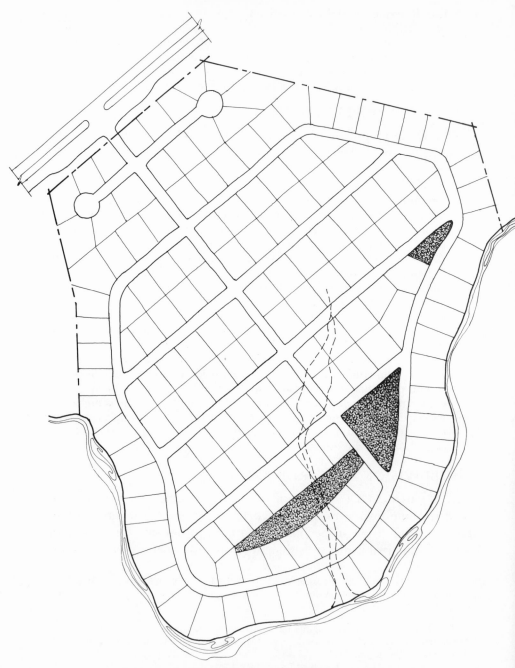

SMALL SUBDIVISION WITH LIMITED OPEN SPACE
APPROXIMATELY 22 ACRES
154 FAMILY UNITS

FIG. 7. Grouping houses in a tighter, more cohesive pattern permits the developer to replace a miscellany of back lots with common parks, playgrounds, and wooded areas.

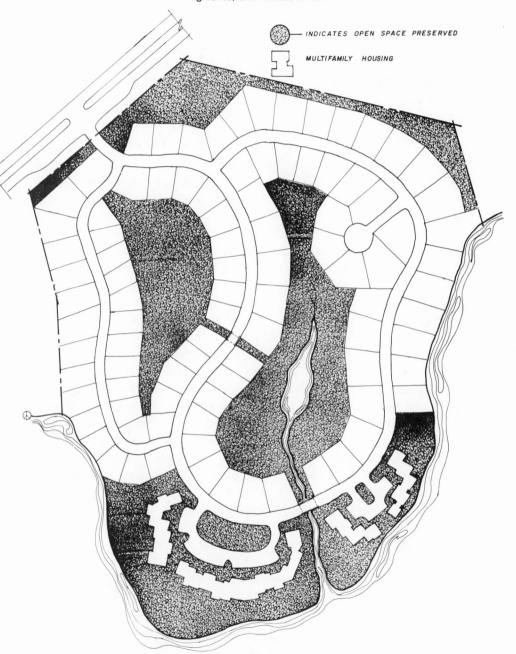

INDICATES OPEN SPACE PRESERVED

MULTIFAMILY HOUSING

SAME SITE WITH ADDITIONAL PLANNED OPEN SPACE

CONNECTING OPEN SPACE CORRIDORS

154 FAMILY UNITS

OFFICIAL MAPPING

Many communities use what is called an official map or community planning map as a control mechanism; the map outlines areas which are to be left open in a community. Although such designations may not be too effective and the ruling may not be held up in court, it does give a planning board or commission some leverage in keeping open land open.[4]

CITIZEN ACTION THROUGH THE COURTS

Rulings on environmental problems are not new to courtrooms in America. Government agencies have long been able to press for certain property rights with the help of the courts, and private property owners have also gone to the courts to settle land grievances. The idea, however, of a new kind of a lawsuit by private citizens' groups to achieve environmental redress is a fairly recent development and quite novel. As Joseph L. Sax, Professor of Law at the University of Michigan, points out, these new lawsuits are characterized by three facts: "First, the plaintiffs are private citizens, not public agencies. Second, they sue not as property owners nor as protectors of any conventional private interest, but as members of the general public asserting rights claimed simply as members of the public. And finally, the defendants are the very government agencies that are supposed to be protecting the public interests."[5] Professor Sax, who has written a book on environmental litigation to be published in 1971, goes on to say that "these new cases arise in many contexts, such as suits against a highway department to challenge the location of a new road or against a pollution control agency for not enforcing the law adequately." A private industry or utility company may be sued to enjoin its plans for locating a new plant or transmission line.[6]

In recent years the National Audubon Society has sued several government agencies where environmental issues were at stake. In 1967 it brought an unprecedented suit against the Army Corps of Engineers enjoining them from diverting additional water from the Everglades National Park. The lawsuit was finally settled successfully out of court. Since that historic case (C-111), the Society has launched half a dozen other suits against government agencies or their officials involving en-

---

[4] See *ibid.*, p. 41, for additional information.
[5] "Legal Redress of Environmental Disruption," *Forum*, May, 1970, p. 50.
[6] *Ibid.*, p. 50.

vironmental matters. Many other cases can be cited of private groups instituting and successfully winning lawsuits against government agencies where environmental damage was at issue. To help private groups with environmental litigation, several private legal groups have been formed, the most noteworthy being the Environmental Defense Fund.[7] The Center for Law and Social Policy, located in Washington, D.C., is another such group.

THE NATURE CENTER APPROACH TO URBAN OPEN LAND

The only real means that any community has for keeping urban land open in the long run lies in the attitudes and actions of its citizens. If citizens are conscious of the value and need for open space, for more nature around them and in their lives, ways and means will be found to keep a certain amount of greenspace viable in a community. If they know little and care less about nature, natural beauty, and other natural amenities, all the zoning and ordinances in the world will not preserve their greenspace for long. This is perhaps one of the reasons why the urban nature center concept now seems to be such a popular idea in this country. Many believe that if open land is to remain a part of the urban American setting, nature appreciation and natural area awareness must be made part of the lives of American city-dwellers.

The nature center concept is aimed at the urban dweller. It is in a sense a new approach to the development of environmental awareness for millions of urban people everywhere.[8] America today has some five hundred urban nature centers (including closely related facilities) but needs two thousand—one for each community of a hundred thousand people. The development of these nature centers would in themselves and in the aggregate help to keep a certain amount of urban land open and would help develop citizen consciousness in each generation to see that man's kinship with nature is not lost. So significant can the concept become in open space preservation in America that we will examine it more closely.

An oasis of green in or around a city just cannot be locked up and unused. The belief that all one needs to do is retire open land, keep it

[7] For further information contact Environmental Defense Fund, Room 9, P.O.B. 740, Stony Brook, N.Y.

[8] See Joseph J. Shomon, "Nature Centers—One Approach to Environmental Education," *Environmental Education Journal* 1 (1969): 56–60.

unused, and all will be well is unrealistic. Some kind of use must be considered, but how much use and under what circumstances? Effective planning for limited development is important, and nature centers offer an excellent option for such development.

No area of urban open land can be everything to everybody. Certain uses are suitable to urban nature centers; others are not. Generally speaking, the following compatible and non-compatible uses are recognized:

Compatible Uses

organized, naturalist-led walks (for school groups)
self-guided walks
organized outdoor education tours (adult groups)
indoor and outdoor lectures
nature and ecological studies
land and water conservation practices
nature painting, photography, sketching, writing
conservation meetings, forums, programs
training workshops for teachers and youth leaders
land laboratory activities
ecological research
educational day camping

Non-Compatible Uses

hunting and fishing
trailer camping, overnight tent camping (except for Scouts
    and then only in a designated area)
motor vehicle use
display of caged mammals and birds
picnicking (except in designated area)
horseback riding
swimming
collecting natural materials, except under special guidance
    from a center naturalist
dog training

PARKING. Well-planned parking space in a nature center area serves several additional functions: it can be a limitation on the carrying capacity of an area, and it can regulate traffic flow and control in an outdoor facility.

BUILDINGS. The character, layout, and extent of buildings can be and very often is a major factor in the preservation of open land. A small, fifty-acre, fragile natural area should usually have its buildings planned close to the main entranceway or gate. Prudence dictates that where possible facilities such as buildings and parking lots should be located so as to conserve the land and its biota.

ROADS AND TRAILS. There is an unfortunate tendency today in outdoor recreation development toward maximum use rather than optimum use. Often we see more roads and trails than are needed or can be adequately maintained. A road should be planned only to meet a vital need. What is true of roads is even more true of so-called nature trails. Generally speaking, urban open recreational areas have too many trails. Often those trails are not well planned or not planned at all; they are often poorly maintained. A trail system should be the heart of any outdoor interpretive area. The visitor should spend a minimum of time in the interpretive building and a maximum of time outdoors. Trails should be designed to satisfy the needs of both the casual and the serious visitor. For the casual visitor a short main conservation trail is desirable; it provides general information about the overall area and shows its basic ecological relationships. With this one main trail in place, loops for specialized study by the more serious visitor can be added. Usually each loop has a primary purpose and is indicated by a loop name. No restrictions are implied here, however, for loop trails are open to the casual visitor as well.

The trail system suggested in Fig. 8 indicates desirable general location and layout with respect to the interpretive building. The final layout, however, should be directed by a professional naturalist. Large trees in the path of the trail system should be removed only when it is impractical to construct around them or when they pose a danger to walkers. Brush and logs cleared from the trail in the building process should not be burned but stacked into large piles at some distance from the trail to serve as a shelter for wildlife. Trees and shrubs should be cut close to the ground and all stumps cleared from the trail area.[9] With eight to ten station stops, various conservation and natural resources relationships can be stressed, either by the naturalist leading tours or in descriptive pamphlets for self-guided trips.

9 For additional information, see *Trail Planning and Layout*, available from the National Audubon Society.

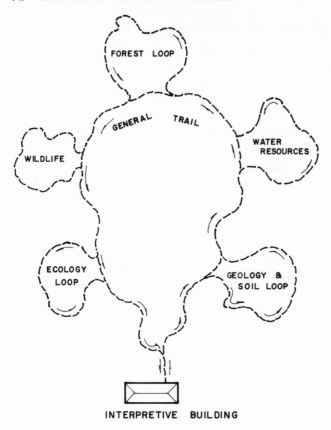

FOREST LOOP

GENERAL TRAIL

WILDLIFE

WATER RESOURCES

ECOLOGY LOOP

GEOLOGY & SOIL LOOP

INTERPRETIVE BUILDING

FIG. 8

A *forestry loop* can illustrate such forest values as shade, climate control, watershed protection, fire control, and seasonal design and the beauty of color. The benefits of sound forestry practices and the multiple-use concept could be effectively demonstrated along this loop.

A *wildlife loop* should be designed to introduce the visitor to as many forms of wildlife as possible.[10] Opportunities to see or hear wildlife can be increased by improving food and water conditions and providing protection and shelter for particular species. Simple habitat improvements, such as hollow logs, nesting trees, thickets, and plant diversity, can greatly increase the number and variety of wildlife in the area.

[10] For more specific information on this subject, see Joseph J. Shomon, Byron L. Ashbaugh, and Con Tolman, *Wildlife Habitat Improvement* (New York: National Audubon Society, Nature Center Planning Division, 1966).

An ecology loop. It is not easy on any one trail to unveil the many ecological relationships that exist in an urban open land area. A special *ecology loop,* however, can do wonders when planned well. Often a stump, rock, stream bank, or pool of water can show what niches and microhabitats are like. An anthill or a bees' nest reveal the colonial life of lower animals.

A touch-and-see trail is primarily designed for the blind and deaf, although the mentally handicapped and wheelchair groups—those who normally have little opportunity to explore or experience the outdoors —can use it effectively. The exact nature and extent of this trail cannot be adequately described here, but by working closely with nearby institutions and schools for the handicapped the naturalist can develop a most instructive special trail.

INTERPRETIVE FEATURES. One of the principal interpretive features commonly found at an urban nature center or in an urban outdoor natural area is the *interpretive building,* serving as an information, orientation and service center. Other outdoor interpretive features which are useful in the urban nature center are a *council ring,* a simple outdoor facility where groups can meet before a trail tour, or at mid-point on a tour, or after a trip has been completed; a *weather station,* which is a small but officially approved weather station located near the interpretive building;[11] a *sundial;*[12] a *bird feeder* with a bird bath and dripping water, which is screened with shrubs on one side in semicircular fashion, yet visible from the building; a *tree stump and mounted log display,* which can be a tree stump with a sloping cut, smoothed and waterproofed to show wood structures and used to point out different functions of sapwood and heartwood as well as interesting periods of history related to specific annual rings; *blinds* constructed of plant materials or woven redwood panels, which can be located in different habitats for wildlife study and photography; an *emergency fire tool box,* a metal display box containing tools for fighting forest fires set on four treated posts, which can help tell the story of forest fire prevention and control and can also be used in emergencies; *observation towers, natural overlooks,* etc., which most visitors to urban nature centers and natural areas enjoy climbing.

The urban nature center approach is a basic one because it builds citizen awareness of and sensitivity to the values of open land preserva-

---

[11] For information on how to set up a weather station write to Environmental Services Administration, Weather Bureau, U.S. Department of Commerce, Washington, D.C.

[12] Directions for constructing a sundial from scrap material are given in circular 402, *Sundials,* available from the U.S. Government Printing Office for 5 cents.

tion; but there are other steps that can be taken to ensure that open land will remain open. Nothing helps to preserve an area better than good management and effective maintenance. One of the easiest ways to lose a park is to let it run down. Then there is always the threat of damage from fire, wild and domestic animals, vandalism, and ineffectual controls over human use. These topics are touched upon in the following chapters.

VI | Administration, Management, Controls, and Maintenance of Open Lands

ADMINISTRATION

LAND RESOURCES ADMINISTRATION is usually carried on by government (federal, state, and local), quasi-public institutions or bodies, or private organizations. This discussion applies to all three types of organizations. A number of types of private open lands, including nature centers, nature preserves, and wildlife sanctuaries, have been developed. Sample constitutions and bylaws, as well as articles of incorporation, are available from various sources.[1]

PERSONNEL

Today most government and private organizations, including industry, are fully cognizant of personnel standards, of proper personnel in-

[1]See appendixes in Byron L. Ashbaugh, *Planning a Nature Center* (New York: National Audubon Society, 1963), pp. 78–83.

doctrination, and of the importance of in-service training. In private land use projects, such as environmental education centers, it has been found that the key to success nearly always is a competent board of directors and a qualified administrative director. Too frequently people in charge of such facilities have no experience in handling land resources. The director of any sort of land-for-learning facility must not only be a good land manager but also a good administrator and a competent teacher.[2]

BUDGETARY FACTORS

Financial limitations are a serious impediment to action programs. Money is not usually easy to come by. Efforts to get sufficient funds for a city or county park interpretive program may be frustrated because priority has been given such items as new buildings and structures or new equipment. Too often money is available for pretentious buildings and structures and not for qualified personnel and adequate maintenance. Stan Ernst, Director of Interpretive Services, Maryland National Capital Parks, Montgomery County, Maryland, points out the need for "balance" in urban land management programs. Ernst's exemplary program shows balanced budgeting for capital outlay, adequate personnel services, and good maintenance. The Montgomery park system is one of the best run in the nation. An example of a private urban facility where there has been good budgeting is the Kalamazoo Nature Center, Kalamazoo, Michigan. Its director, Dr. Lewis Batts, has seen to it that facilities and services are in balance. The St. Louis Botanical Garden and the Morton Arboretum are two other good examples of well-managed private urban institutions carrying out excellent land-for-learning programs.

MANAGEMENT

Modern natural resources management, whether by government or private organizations, implies two types of control—that over the land itself and over the users of the resource. There is most assuredly such a thing as an "ecological relationship" in the use of land and water and its accompanying life. No longer can one form of land use ignore

[2] For help on how to obtain qualified people for nature center facilities, write to the National Audubon Society, Nature Center Planning Division; see also *Directory of Environmental Education Facilities* (New York: National Audubon Society, Nature Center Planning Division, 1969).

another. Overgrazing a hillside affects water quantity and quality. Motorization can limit the value of a city park. So-called ecological management is becoming more and more important in national and state forests, wildlife refuges, and game management areas. For example, in the Virginia Massanutten project of the U.S. Forest Service (covering some hundred thousand acres), the main planned usage is outdoor interpretive education and recreation; all other uses and management measures are subordinated to these.[3] No trees, for example, are to be harvested where outdoor recreation and aesthetics are the prime values. This kind of ecological management should be used more extensively in the natural lands of urban areas. A park that is too heavily manicured, like Prospect Park in Brooklyn, is not only likely to displease those with an eye trained to look for ecological

[3] See the case study in Chapter XI.

values but is damaging to the natural relationships of the area itself. More and more activities such as timber harvesting along highways and roadsides, "chaining" of pinyon juniper cover on western mountain slopes (which can be easily seen by the visitor), and chemical poisoning of whole forest ecosystems to attain forest monoculture are being re-examined. Ecological management may also mean using natural means (fire rather than chemicals, for example) to control certain kinds of vegetation and to favor others. It also includes greater reliance on biotic controls in insects, with one species helping to control another, and as well as leaving entire plant communities untouched so that nature can do her best work.

CONTROLS

FIRE CONTROL. Urban open land is particularly vulnerable to wild fire. Most wild fires are caused by man, but some are caused by lightning. A good fire-fighting plan that outlines preventive measures as well as actual steps to be followed when a fire breaks out is important. Federal and state forest agencies can provide help on fire plans. Extra precautionary measures must be taken in urban lands because they are so vulnerable to fires set by humans and because of their prime value to such large numbers of people. Schuylkill Valley Nature Center in the Germantown section of Philadelphia, a well-planned facility, has been repeatedly burned over, and as a result the area is not nearly as attractive as it could be. Fire, however, is not all bad; under controlled conditions it can be a useful tool in both plant and wildlife management. In southern pinelands, for example, it is difficult to get longleaf pine to sprout without a surface fire. Very often, too, wildlife habitat improvement measures can be effected with controlled burning.

CONTROLS OVER ANIMALS. Damage by domestic livestock and dogs and cats is sometimes observed. The best immediate response to such damage is to contact the agency responsible for the type of animal control involved. Fencing sometimes is needed. As more land goes into monoculture (raising of single crops on a large scale), damage from wild animals, such as voles and certain birds, is likely to become more acute. One valuable aspect of urban open space is to give some ecological balance to a monocultural environment by preserving natural communities in an area.

CONTROLS OVER HUMAN USE. Damage caused by the numbers of human beings on the land is a matter of growing concern to land managers. The "carrying capacity" of the land is a concept that must apply to humans as well as animals. A given parcel of land can only support or accommodate so many people (or animals) at any one time, as well as over any period of time. The problem is one of determining what the human carrying capacities are for an area and then seeing to it that those capacities are not exceeded. A good control device in many situations that has been mentioned is the design of a parking lot. If a park or nature center has a limited capacity, people not finding parking space can be urged to return at another hour or another day. A bridge designed to allow only so many people to pass over it (to an island or swamp) in any given period is another example of a measure to limit the number of persons in a fragile area. Such bridges are best designed for one-way traffic.

CONTROL OF VANDALISM

Destruction or injury to open lands and the various facilities on them is a major problem. Vandalism cuts heavily into operating budgets, disrupts planning and operations, and lessens the enjoyment which people can derive from an area. It can best be dealt with when the underlying causes are understood. Traditional methods of control, largely those of prevention and protection, have been ineffective simply because so little attention has been given to why people resort to vandalism.

Vandalism manifests itself in two forms: the willful destruction or defacing of property and damage caused by ignorance. Both create equally great problems. Of the two forms, willful vandalism is the most serious. Such acts are expressions of deep-seated frustrations stemming from social and economic inequalities. Until we can relieve these frustrations in more acceptable ways (or remove their causes), we shall have to depend largely on superficial stopgap measures. One helpful step, however, is getting the vandals involved in the very project that they are vandalizing—preferably before they become vandals. This approach has occasionally been extremely successful, and a good example is the fine work being done with youth at the Stark Wilderness Center, Canton, Ohio.

Vandalism through ignorance is less difficult to control, although here again, the traditional methods are not the most effective. Generally speaking, a large share of the trouble is caused by people who "should know better" but who, through carelessness, thoughtlessness, or lack of guidance, destroy and deface property. Educational programs, both formal and informal, can effectively reduce the incidence of this kind of vandalism. Formal education programs that help are aimed at school classes and various youth and adult clubs and organizations. Slide shows, films, and lectures can be used to develop attitudes of respect and appreciation for public and private property. Informal programs use the mass media toward the same end. Television and radio commercials, posters and signs, and statements by popular public figures help to bring public attention to the problem.

Prompt maintenance is another proven method of reducing the incidence of vandalism. Defaced or damaged property, if not promptly repaired, invites further damage. Very few people are willing to cast the first stone or carve the first inscription, but once it begins, more

Vandalism such as the destruction of park property shown here is often an expression of personal and social frustration. It is by no means a simple problem to solve. One interesting way of dealing with it is to involve youngsters actively in the very project they are vandalizing—preferably before patterns of destructive behavior become established.

quickly follows. The answer here is to maintain the property in such a state of repair and tidiness that a person will think twice before resorting to minor acts of vandalism.

Another innovative method of preventing vandalism before it begins is situational control, for example, the planting of brambles around a restricted area or along a path, which has been highly effective wherever it has been wisely planned. People are less apt to cross such a barrier. At Port Charlotte, Florida, an attractive, artificially made hillock has been planted with some interesting semitropical plants. They can be viewed easily from a nearby path, but a barrier of yucca plantings is an effective barrier to those few who might wish to leave the path and climb the hill.

The personnel operating a facility are invaluable in stemming vandalism. Staff members who are sensitive to the problem and able to communicate with offenders in a rational manner are more effective than those who are inflexible or dogmatic. Through wise handling an

Projects such as the stream erosion control work shown here can result in improvements to open land as well as in reduction of vandalism. (Photo Wisconsin Conservation Department, Madison, Wisconsin.)

offender can become a strong future ally. In a nature center in New Haven, Connecticut, Anthony Cozenza has done a fine job by enlisting the help of would-be vandals: he has organized teenage boys (including some who have been in trouble) to develop and operate a small nature center. Finally, a word must be said in favor of rules and regulations. Most people do not object to rules when they are well presented, and a clear and sensible set of rules, intelligently enforced, is extremely helpful in preventing vandalism.

MAINTENANCE

It is always better policy to prevent something unwanted from happening than to wrestle with the problem after it arises. This is the principle followed in *preventive* maintenance—you prevent the breakdown before it occurs. For example, the roof of a building begins to develop a small leak; the sensible thing to do is to repair the spot before extensive decay sets in and a whole roof needs replacing. A dying tree along a nature trail can be removed promptly, while it is firm and intact, at minimum expense. Several years later, after dangerous limbs and snags have developed, the job is more costly, more complicated. If the public begins to make its own criss-cross trails through an area, such misuses should be hit quickly and hard before permanent damage occurs and correction becomes a big job. Other examples of good preventive maintenance are the keeping up of fences, upkeep of roads and walkways and trails, proper greasing of vehicles, regular painting, and so on. Preventive maintenance not only is a sign of good management but is also good business and sound economics.

A noticeable weakness in many present-day land use operations, especially where heavy human use is a factor, is poor or improper maintenance of facilities, equipment, and grounds. American affluence and pursuit of a way of life that favors built-in obsolescence of products certainly helps to undermine our appreciation of the importance of effective maintenance, and here both government and private facilities often suffer from this attitude. Most big-city parks, like Central Park in New York, are poorly maintained. Private facilities most often are better maintained, although this is not always the case. Often a situation must get so bad that the public is aroused and demands that something be done before action is taken. Such was the case with many of our national parks after World War II: in some places parks and facilities had to be closed down. Only when there was a public uproar were funds voted to correct the situation and the parks reopened.

Land resource administrators and managers as a rule must become more conscious of good maintenance and assign it a higher level of priority in management. Generally speaking, the public wants it and is willing to pay the cost. While not glamorous, it is as important as new structures and innovative facilities. Harold Wallin, chief naturalist of the Cleveland Metropolitan Park District, points to two factors that save money in his park system, good maintenance and an effective outdoor interpretive program. "These actually pay off," Wallin says: "in fact, we couldn't operate our parks without these two vital functions." Byron L. Ashbaugh, former chief planner of the National Audubon Society and a well-known specialist in outdoor interpretive education, makes a strong case for maintenance throughout his excellent guidebook *Trail Planning and Layout*. He stresses that no outdoor area can be effective without constant attention to maintenance of facilities and land.[4]

---

[4] This 104-page guidebook is available from the National Audubon Society, Nature Center Planning Division.

VII | Economic, Social, and Political Considerations

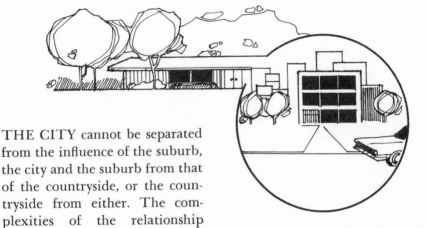

THE CITY cannot be separated from the influence of the suburb, the city and the suburb from that of the countryside, or the countryside from either. The complexities of the relationship between man's environment and his social order are beginning to be recognized. The ecology of man, geoecology, and bioecology are all interwoven. To keep our urban environments from becoming impossible and unmanageable, we must consider the socioeconomic and political forces that are constantly at work in them.

ECONOMIC FACTORS

In New York City a six-block ghetto area is being demolished in an apparent effort to improve the environment of its boxed-in inhabitants. Instead of providing more elbow room, however, the city is allowing the area to be developed as another high-density tenement complex. Will this kind of treatment improve the inner-city human environment in the long run? Why must it be more apartments? Why cannot it be more open space, more greenery, perhaps a well-planned park for the people who live in congested surrounding neighborhoods and who need a measure of relief from tensions and monotony? Can New York or any other huge city survive with more crowding?[1] More than likely

[1] For a revealing insight of the effects of crowding on animals, see Edward T. Hall's *The Hidden Dimension* (Garden City, N.Y.: Doubleday & Co., 1967).

85

these questions will remain unanswered, and this particular development (which is a private one) will be governed largely by the immediate economic return to the developer.

A decent urban life demands that the extra people we have there and will continue to have for some time (although efforts at population control are essential and are beginning to pay dividends) must be provided for in other settings—greater densities in the suburbs, as we see in some European satellite cities, or new towns and cities in the hinterlands. A central issue today is the conflict between long-range benefits for the many and immediate profits for the few. Modern developers often do not see the possibilities of other options in land use and development. Were they to offer the city several alternatives, including those with high social values, cities like New York and others might be able to resolve their ever more serious dilemma. In growth, development, and redevelopment there are values other than dollars and profits—far-reaching social and intangible values. Moreover, some effort should be made to *contain* growth. When nature and breathing space begin to compete with the profit motive on the planning and design table, as Lawrence Halprin argues, we will be on the road toward an improved urban environment. "We do have a clear image of the purpose of an ideal city," Halprin says: "This purpose is clearly to make possible a rich and biologically satisfying life for all the city's people."[2] As in the case of environmental pollution, short-term economic gains must give way to the greater requirements of society. What created our present-day dilemma, among other things, was our attention to the profit motive without regard to the long-term social implications of our actions. Now a realignment of socioeconomic values becomes a necessity.

TAXATION. Taxation is a powerful tool in the shaping and design of cities, as well as controlling their growth through the use of open land. Taxation, according to William I. Goodman, is also thought to be a factor in "influencing development decisions as well as providing incentives for the retention of open land in undeveloped uses."[3] The accepted notion (although not necessarily always true) is that taxes force land into development. Many local governments are using taxation to effect low-density levels and to keep more open land open. Through such measures as tax exemptions, tax deferments, preferential assess-

[2] *Cities* (New York: Reinhold Publishing Corporation, 1963), p. 7.
[3] Goodman and Freund, eds., *Principles and Practice of Urban Planning*, p. 204.

ment, deferral, and differential rates, many municipalities are able to keep underdeveloped land open.[4]

Exemption. Public open space—parks and public conservation areas —are usually exempt from property taxation. The partial or full exemption of private open space lands is commonly determined by their benefit or use to the public. "These benefits are not just for the users of the facilities, but for adjacent areas as well where amenities and real estate values have been boosted."[5]

Preferential Assessment. Preferential tax assessment for agriculture is a device to encourage the continuation of farming by keeping agricultural land assessed at its agricultural value rather than at its development value. The high assessments of undeveloped land in the urban fringes, usually based on development values, have forced farmers to succumb to the tempting offers of land speculators. This has occurred, for example, in Nassau and Suffolk counties in New York State. Orange County, New York, on the other hand, is trying to keep most of its area rural by encouraging agricultural zoning. In Maryland preferential tax assessment in Prince Georges and Montgomery counties has not worked out that way. Farming has continued in many cases, but many farmers and farm owners are now themselves speculators, profiting from the tax benefits and looking forward to the day when their hayfields and cornfields will be covered with houses. Certainly there are instances where owner-operators have benefited from the tax relief, but on the whole the Maryland preferential tax assessment has not solved the problem, and reduced tax rates alone have not prevented unwanted suburbanization.

Deferral. A second tax scheme aimed at preserving open space uses like farming and also at overcoming the deficiencies of the Maryland program is a tax deferral system for open land. In 1965 the Northern Virginia Regional Planning and Economic Development Commission proposed that

> under a tax deferral system, all taxes on land, located within a *planned or an existing open space site*, would be deferred as long as it remains in an open type land use (taxes on improvements would still be collected).

[4] An excellent pamphlet by John E. Rickert, "The Present and Potential Role of State and Local Taxation in the Preservation or Development of Open Space Land in Urban Fringe Areas" (unpublished manuscript, Urban Land Institute, December, 1965), discusses the utility of these different methods of taxation in detail.

[5] Goodman and Freund, *Principles and Practice of Urban Planning*, p. 204.

However, if an owner of such a site decides to develop for a non-open space use then all deferred taxes would have to be paid before a sub-division plan or building permits would be issued. If the property is sold the tax lien goes with it and the market price should be reduced by the amount of the tax lien. If the land is subdivided and sold but not developed the tax lien is proportioned, based on the size of the subdivided parcels. . . . If the public eventually buys the land, the deferred tax would reduce the market value of the property and could be considered as installment payments on the property.[6]

This scheme has a precedent in the Commonwealth of Virginia, where a forest yield tax is administered by the Department of Conservation and Economic Development. Here the idea is to suspend taxes on all forest land suited for timber growth when it is offered as a temporary reserve for wildlife or recreation, but the forest yield taxes must be paid at the time of cutting, when the landowner can bear the burden. The chief objective of this program is to stop the practice of premature cutting. This open land deferral idea for the sale of agricultural lands, with its penalty of payment of back taxes, provides a better method than Maryland's preferential tax assessment for retaining open space.

Just how much of a burden back taxes will be for an investor or builder who anticipates hundreds of thousands of dollars of profit is uncertain. A developer could quickly recover the payment of back taxes by raising the price of each house by a hundred dollars or by charging a few dollars more per square foot in a commercial building. Tax deferral nevertheless is a device to be encouraged in open land programs, as it is an inducement to owners to keep land open. This is particularly true of owners of recreation facilities like golf courses, riding stables, or lakes, who are trying to hold on to their property in the face of soaring taxes. The system, however, will work only when tied to other land use controls like zoning and acquisition. Alone, it will have small effectiveness in preserving open land.

SOCIAL CONSIDERATIONS

It is said that management of natural resources is 90 per cent man-agement of people. Conservation administrators often point out that it is the attitudes of citizens which cause them concern, for through their ballots they either support or wreck a program. Without at least a measure of understanding of why people change and what motivates

---

[6] Unpublished Commission report, quoted in *ibid.,* p. 205.

them, we are reduced to bungling and guesswork in the management of our natural resources, often with dire consequences to the community, state, and nation. There are many hypotheses about the causes and character of attitudes toward natural resources and about the measurement of these attitudes, but such a discussion belongs to a more academic treatise. This complex subject challenges even behavioral scientists who specialize in such inquiries. What is attempted here is a brief review of how attitudes are formed, what motivates people, and how attitudes can be changed.

There is nothing truly stationary in the world. Change is an established phenomenon, the law of the universe. Raymond B. Fosdick well expressed the concept some years ago:

> When the last glacier retreated northward from what is now Connecticut it left behind, as mementoes of its visit, great boulders of rock which are now strewn lavishly across the state. Several of them, as large as a corncrib and many tons in weight, were deposited on my farm, and for fifteen years I have watched one of them fight a losing battle with an ash tree. The tree evidently started in a seed lodged in a tiny pocket in the tip of the rock. When I first saw it, it was a sturdy sapling that had made for itself a comfortable crevice for its roots. Today its irresistible growth has torn the massive rock into fragments.
>
> This is the law of life. The future belongs not to rigid absolutes, whether they are primal rocks or unyielding social arrangements, but to the thing that can grow, whether it is a tree or a democracy.[7]

Like all things, human beings change. How easily and how quickly they do so depends largely upon their culture. It rests with each generation of humans to change its attitudes and its actions for the better.

The branch of social science known as group dynamics focuses on social change. Studies in group dynamics show certain principles to be operating whenever a change in people takes place. Dorwin Cartwright lists eight such principles:

1. If the group is to be used effectively as a medium of change, those people who are to be changed and those who are to exert influence for change must have a strong sense of belonging to the same group.
2. The more attractive the group is to its members, the greater is the influence that it can exert on them.

7 "We Must Not Be Afraid of Change," *New York Times Magazine*, April 3, 1949, p. 7.

3. In attempts to change attitudes, values, or behavior, the more relevant they are to the basis for the group's appeal to its members, the greater is the group's influence on them.

4. The greater the prestige of a group member is in the eyes of the other members, the greater is the influence he can exert.

5. Efforts to change individuals or members of sub-groups within a group which, if successful, would make them deviate from the norms of the group will encounter strong resistance.

6. Change can be effected by creating a shared perception of the need for such change, thus making the group itself the source of pressure for change.

7. Information relating to the need for change, plans for change, and the consequences of change must be shared by all relevant people in the group.

8. Changes in one part of a group produce strain in other parts, which can be reduced only by eliminating the change or by bringing about readjustments in the related parts.[8]

How do individuals and groups develop attitudes? Why do they have certain opinions, certain beliefs?[9] Some facts are well established: attitudes are largely a product of the surrounding culture and come from the environment; attitudes are formed early in life, usually during the formative years of training; attitudes strongly entrenched cannot be changed readily, but they can be changed; attitudes are largely formed through personal experience, with strong reinforcement from training; attitudes are expressed in countless fashions, shade into one another, and are stratified as society is stratified but may be readily distorted.

Basically, man is motivated by two main drives, the so-called biological or hereditary drive and the environmental drive. The first includes the natural inheritance of man, such as the pressure for survival, food, and sex. The second includes the whole gamut of pressures from the environment, the social system, or the conditions under which one lives—the desire for security, popularity, personal and social recognition, and social acceptance.

---

[8] Dorwin Cartwright, "Achieving Change in People," *Human Relations* 4 (1951): 387–91.

[9] According to sociologists, only individuals can have "opinions" and "beliefs." A "public," which is said to be a group of people associated by some common bond, cannot have an opinion because it is not an entity in itself. "Public opinion" is simply the collective opinion of individuals.

BIOPOLITICS

Whether they represent planning groups, architects, zoning boards, government agencies, or private conservation groups, organizations and individuals who seek the preservation and wise use of natural environments in urban America must involve themselves in biopolitics. The safekeeping of a salubrious environment is as much a political struggle as a battle against traditional land misuse.

Edward Kozicky, former president of The Wildlife Society, in an address to wildlife biologists, recently explained the need for political involvement on the part of his audience:

> Biopolitics is the art of combining modern game management with the political facts of life. It is necessary that the modern wildlife administrator be an expert biopolitician.
>
> Today, trained biologists probe deeper and deeper with better tools, into the lives and times of various game species. The land and water habitats that produce our game are constantly changing, with ever-increasing demands being made on the landscape by an expanding human population.
>
> To work effectively, biologists need freedom from political whims and problems. Their main role is a relentless pursuit for biological facts, so that truth can replace fallacy in the management of our game species.
>
> But there is frustration among some biologists—especially recent graduates. They discover new facts, and expect to see their findings acted upon immediately. When this doesn't happen, they feel defeated, and conclude that they are nothing more than political pawns or are working for a group of knot-headed administrators.
>
> By nature, the American public is slow to accept change. Most of us even resent change. Hence, it does take a lot of educational selling to promote a new concept that may not be spectacular, such as habitat improvement.
>
> Regardless of how free any fish and game department may be of politics, it still must work with the representatives of the people—the state legislature. Without the legislators' support, no conservation program can succeed.
>
> Hence, every progressive fish and game department is engaged in biopolitics, and this fact of life must be recognized as a necessity in our democracy and appreciated by every conservation employee.[10]

Kozicky's comments also apply to those working in the field of urban open land preservation. Biopolitics is one tool that must be mastered in order to put worthy programs into action.

[10] *The Wildlife Society News*, June, 1969.

VIII | The City and the
Megalopolis:
Case Studies

MANY COMMUNITIES have dealt successfully with the problem of urban open land preservation. This chapter and the two that follow give the reader a quick overview of a few outstanding projects, ranging from the large city and the megalopolis to suburban areas and the countryside. The case studies I have chosen are geographically widespread and are those with which I am personally familiar.

COLUMBUS, OHIO

One of the most notable programs of urban open land preservation involving city park lands is to be found in Columbus, Ohio. Here the work of the Metropolitan Park District, under the dynamic leadership of such men as Walter Tucker, has produced a city and a metropolitan

93

open lands and parks system perhaps second to none in the United States.

BACKGROUND. In 1917 the Ohio Legislature made it possible for local communities to establish park districts. The law was the culmination of early efforts by Ohio conservationists to preserve natural lands in and around urban areas. The Ohio Park District law produced dramatic results in the state not only because it focused sharply on an important need but also because it provided the machinery to do the job. Autonomous boards were created to administer the affairs of the park districts: they were given limited taxing powers for operational funds and authority to acquire lands for the conservation of natural resources and to promote the use of such lands for the general welfare.

The Columbus Metropolitan Park District was created on August 14, 1945, and its board received its first funds on January 1, 1947. Since then, the park system has grown to seven reservations (or parks) with a total area of over 5,604 acres. Three of the parks are developed and open to the public. Four are under development and still restricted (as of 1970) to limited public use. The parks provide outdoor recreation annually for hundreds of thousands of people. Facilities for public use include picnic grounds, large playing fields, woodland trails, and specially designed facilities for group use, day camps, and outdoor schools.

The Ohio Park District law provided for the creation of park districts, the appointment of park commissioners, the naming of a secretary and the employment of a staff; it also defined the board's taxing power and authorized it to acquire property, to establish rules and regulations, and to police its lands. The law further gave the districts the power to develop and promote the use of their lands. The affairs of each district are administered by a board of three commissioners appointed for overlapping three-year terms by a judge of the Probate Court. The commissioners serve without pay. The board is a corporate body and may sue and be sued.

FINANCING THE PARK DISTRICT. The Ohio Park District law provides that to support their operations metropolitan park boards may levy a tax, not to exceed one-half mill in any one year, on all taxable property within a park district. Should additional funds be needed, the law provides that park boards may submit to the voters the question of levying an additional tax, not to exceed three-tenths of a mill in any one year. All funds under the control of a park board are kept in depositories selected by the board and secured as required by law. Such funds are disbursed upon order of the board as evidenced by the certificate of the secretary. The Columbus Metropolitan Park Board submits a budget to the budget commission each year equal to a levy of about one-tenth of a mill. In addition to its tax-free funds, the park district receives some income from permit fees and charges for services which are used for maintenance expenses. Additional revenue is derived from the sale of refreshments and from the rental of undeveloped properties.

THE REGIONAL CONCEPT. From the beginning the Columbus Park Board has recognized that sound planning is essential for communities seeking to establish park goals, policies, and standards; to formulate sound acquisition and development programs; to prepare a capital improvements program; and to apply for federal grants-in-aid. When population growth and rapid urbanization in the Columbus area indicated a need for a wider approach to park planning than afforded by city planning alone—one reflecting overall needs of the corporate and non-corporate parts of the city—a regional approach was adopted. Accordingly, the master plans of the Columbus Metropolitan Park District were included in the official comprehensive plan of the Columbus and Franklin County Regional Planning Commission.

With open land fast disappearing and land values increasing, the Columbus Metropolitan Park Board gave first priority to land acquisition. In pursuing this program it saw the advisability of concentrating on a few sites but making them larger than originally proposed. Today only one of the seven parks ringing the city falls short of the desired minimum size of five hundred acres.

Although the board set a policy of giving land acquisition precedence over development in the use of funds, it has included some improvements in its budget each year as funds permit. First priority under the heading of improvements went to protection of the properties, followed by reforestation and permanent planting, road construction and improvement, and new construction to expand facilities for public use. The picnic grounds and areas for general public use are maintained in a typical park-like condition, but the woods and natural areas are left more or less untouched. Most natural areas are accessible only by foot trails.

PARK USE AND PROGRAMS. Surveys indicate that the dominant uses of the metropolitan parks are for family picnicking and group outings, with sitting and walking as the most popular activities. Play areas and playground facilities are extensively used by children. Park personnel rank outdoor interpretive education programs high as desirable activities for the public. The value of such programs in reducing vandalism and park misuse was mentioned earlier. Summer and winter programs, including nature walks, and lectures and films on conservation are available to the general public.

Teachers from city and suburban schools utilize the park's forests and ponds for the study of biology, including ecology. In many cases they are assisted by park naturalists. Interpretive buildings, nature trails, a trailside museum, and outdoor classrooms are provided at several of the parks to broaden and deepen the outdoor experience. A number of day camps are also available for use by special groups. Camp programs emphasize outdoor living, nature lore, camping skills, and the appreciation of natural beauty. Several conference and outdoor education centers with overnight facilities are available for the training of leaders in nature interpretation and for outdoor leadership training for camp counselors. The metropolitan parks do not provide overnight or vacation facilities for the general public. This is usually regarded as a proper function of state and national parks.

A total of 4,063,969 visits was reported in the period 1961–1967 for the seven parks which make up the Columbus Metropolitan Park District. Day camps located in six of the parks reported 44,031 camper days in 1967; in the 1961–1967 period a total of 233,766 camper days was reported, involving children in the age group six to fourteen. Over the same seven-year period 72,520 fifth-grade pupils and 27,585 other school children took part in field trips led by naturalists.

The park board and planning staff continue to conduct surveys and studies to improve parklands and to develop a major metropolitan park system. With continued good planning and a forward-looking park board, the prospects for urban open land preservation as well as an excellent park system and a program involving both recreation and education appear to be assured for the Columbus metropolitan area.

NEW YORK'S MAJOR ISLAND OF GREEN

Within ten miles of Times Square and within sight and hearing of the John F. Kennedy International Airport lies an island of land, marshes, and shallow salt water of 18½ square miles—the Jamaica Bay Wildlife Refuge—which is unique in America. The only major wildlife sanctuary in a city of great size, it is accessible to eight million New Yorkers by subway. The preservation of the island of green and the establishment of the wildlife sanctuary by the city park department (now known as the New York City Parks, Recreation and Cultural Affairs Administration) is one of the most notable achievements of urban conservation of our time. Although New York City's five boroughs are blessed with many parks and playgrounds, and, surprisingly, sizeable areas of open space still exist, the Jamaica Bay Wildlife Refuge is the only large city area developed mainly for wildlife.

BACKGROUND. Around the turn of the century Jamaica Bay was largely an unspoiled natural salt marsh bay. The water was clean, fish were abundant, and shellfish were gathered by the tons. As the city grew and development of every kind moved in on the bay, the water became polluted and pollution worsened until all bathing and shellfishing had to be prohibited. During the past half century many schemes for the development and improvement of the bay, some very wild, were proposed.[1] In 1922 a plan was adopted to convert the approximately twelve thousand areas of bay into a huge industrial port with miles of piers and docks. When completed, it would have been larger than the ports of Rotterdam, Hamburg, and Liverpool combined. This project, however, never got beyond the planning stage. In the 1940's another "fantastic" scheme was proposed, the construction of a huge garbage dump in the bay. Proponents of the plan predicted that the area was large enough to handle all of the city's garbage for many years. The ire of Parks Commissioner Robert Moses was aroused, and he had an artist draw up a conception of such a dump. It depicted a mountain of burning garbage belching clouds of smoke over the city. Thanks to Moses' attacks, the dump was never established. Many other plans have been proposed since that time: industrial plants, large housing projects, Coney Island-type development. The bay is also constantly threatened by the expansion of Kennedy airport, and thus the struggle continues.

Since 1950 some progress in reclaiming and improving the bay has been made. Construction of sewage plants has partially corrected the water pollution problem, although much remains to be done. Parks Commissioner Moses decided in 1950 that a bird sanctuary might be established in Jamaica Bay. Various experts in wildlife conservation were consulted, notably Dr. Clarence A. Cottom, then assistant director of the U.S. Fish and Wildlife Service, and a proposal was drawn up. In that year a fire destroyed the trestle which carried the Long

[1] Much of the information given here was prepared by Herbert Johnson, Superintendent of the Jamaica Bay Wildlife Refuge, Box 202, Howard Beach, Jamaica, New York.

Island Railroad to the Rockaways, and this accident turned out to be a blessing for the Jamaica Bay project. The city purchased the old spur, and the New York City Transit Authority decided to dredge up sand from the bay for an embankment or causeway on which to run rapid transit lines to the Rockaways. Because the bay was under the jurisdiction of the New York City Parks Department, it was necessary for the Transit Authority to get permission from that department to dredge. Commissioner Moses granted it with the proviso that the Authority dredge sufficient sand to construct a large land area with two ponds. Dikes were also constructed to lock in two areas of salt water. One impoundment was to be approximately a hundred acres in extent, the second about forty acres. These ponds were completed in the summer of 1953, and the groundwork was laid for a wildlife sanctuary in New York City.

WILDLIFE HABITAT IMPROVEMENT. Under the leadership of Herbert Johnson and a small staff of park assistants, a plan for habitat development was prepared and put into effect. Beach grass was planted on the dredged-up sand of the dikes to prevent wind erosion. Approximately a million and a half beach grass seedlings were planted with a converted cabbage planter. If these plants were placed in a single row, they

The Jamaica Bay Wildlife Refuge is the only large area in New York City developed mainly for wildlife.

would stretch from New York City to Boston. A two-mile walkway loop of blue stone gravel was constructed around the forty-acre impoundment known as West Pond. A parking lot was also built; it has been enlarged twice since construction and will soon have to be enlarged again.

As the higher land consisted entirely of sand, some native grass, and a few bayberry bushes, it was necessary to institute a planting program favorable to wildlife. Plant species were selected that would tolerate the growing conditions as well as providing the maximum amount of food and cover as quickly as possible. Autumn olive, Russian olive, Rugosa rose, chokeberry, wild cherry, bayberry, willow oak, various poplars and willows, Japanese black pine, red cedar, and other species were planted.

As the marshland within the impounded areas stabilized, the original vegetation disappeared. Phragmites and common reed grass soon

FIG. 9

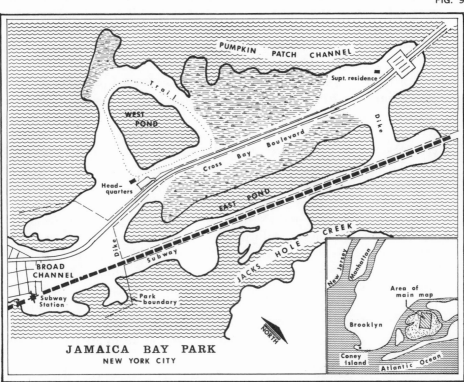

covered the marshy spots and provided excellent cover for nesting waterfowl. Constant mowing of the higher and drier areas resulted in the build-up of turf and the appearance of worms in the soil. In the first six or seven years, a robin was a rare bird in this area, but with the development of the grassy areas and the coming of worms, the robin is now a common nesting bird. Most of the higher land has now been planted with various shrubs and trees and has become a tremendous attraction for land birds.

With the exception of a few oaks, all the plant material was propagated in an established refuge nursery. Japanese black pine seed was obtained from cones of established pine groves on the beaches, and deciduous plant material was propagated from seed and vegetative cuttings. Because the area was sandy, the plants were placed in modest pockets of soil and were quite small when planted. With the aid of fertilizer (when available) the plants have thrived and over the years have contributed their own organic matter to the soil. Despite the artificial plantings, the area looks quite natural. As birds carry many types of seed in their travels, the great influx of bird life has introduced many plant species to the refuge. While most plants are native to the region, two species, foxtail barley and buffalo bur, are new to the area.

VISITATION. Much doubt that a successful bird sanctuary could be developed within ten miles of Times Square was originally expressed. Its success is attested by the visitors that come to the Jamaica Bay Wildlife Refuge each year. The attendance has increased steadily each year, from a few scattered visitors in 1950 to more than seventy-five thousand persons in 1970. The consistent comment of people as they leave the area is that the visit was a source of pleasure and enjoyment. The expert birder is constantly on the lookout for a new or rare bird to add to his life list. The average birder seems to develop new knowledge of birds and nature with each visit. In many cases new visitors had no notion of the charms of bird watching until they came to the refuge. After a few visits the beginning birder purchases a pair of binoculars and a bird book and starts the delightful task of bird identification. Weekend in and weekend out the birders return, in all kinds of weather, in an attempt to add a new bird to their list. The refuge is a meeting ground for people from all walks of life and backgrounds.

During the past fifteen years, 305 bird species have been observed in the refuge. As plant material began to mature the number of nesting birds increased; now more than fifty species nest yearly. A small island in the Bay, Canarsie Pol, contains one of the finest heron rookeries on the Atlantic Coast. Here the snowy and common egrets nest in great numbers, along with many black crowned and yellow crowned night and green herons. Glossy ibis, which first appeared in the refuge in 1962, now nest in great numbers (nearly a hundred pairs each year). Abundant among waterfowl nesters are black duck, mallard, gadwall, redhead, ruddy, and shoveler. Common gallinule, bittern, and several species of rails breed each year. Geese are a common sight at the refuge: at times in the fall and early winter more than seventy-five thousand are there, mostly Canada geese and brant, with some snow geese as well.

Among visitors seen in increasing numbers at the refuge are elderly people, who find the easy walk around the pond a pleasant experience. The path is not too rigorous anywhere, and there are benches available for resting at frequent intervals. While they sit and rest, they enjoy the activity of the birds. There has also been a steady increase in the number of school classes visiting the refuge. In the spring of 1968 at least one class a day, and sometimes two, visited the area. The Parks Department will furnish a guide for a school group when requested to do so. For many children this trip is their first significant introduction to an outdoor nature study area, and certainly their first visit to a bird sanctuary. Urban ecology classes are also coming to the refuge.

FUTURE URBAN OPEN LAND. Much remains to be done at Jamaica Bay—construction of more walks, increased planting, addition of manmade ponds, erection of a small interpretive building. Much needs to be done to control pollution, both air and water, and to preserve the integrity of the area from those who want to dredge and fill. As was pointed out above, however, the greatest struggle for conservationists is against the airport only two miles to the east. The threat of its expanding and engulfing the entire bay is real, and both present and following generations may have to join the battle if the bay and the refuge are to survive.[2]

A MINI-OASIS IN A MEGALOPOLIS

In contrast to New York's major island of green, Manhattan's Paley

[2] As this book went to press, the Port Authority announced that it would abandon its plan for extending runways into the refuge: a National Academy of Sciences study committee issued a report strongly urging against airport expansion.

Park is a man-made pocket of nature of postage-stamp size. Its total area is only 2,520 square feet, and its frontage on Fifty-Third Street, just east of Fifth Avenue, is a mere 42 feet. It is surrounded by towering skyscrapers, noise, gas fumes, and the rush and confusion of a megalopolis. First opened to the public on May 23, 1967, Paley Park is distinctive, not just for its small size but for the concept it represents.

The pebble-strewn earth of the park is shaded by seventeen locust trees. The canopy of locusts, placed at twelve-foot intervals, is planned to give some natural shade over the entire site. Water is fed to the roots of the trees by a special underground system, making it possible to carry the granite paving stones up to the tree trunks. The concrete side walls are covered with Kudzu, and eventually English ivy will be the permanent cover. The waterfall forming the rear wall of the park helps cut down strident traffic noise. Twenty feet high and as wide as the

Even a small oasis, like New York City's Paley Park, can be a blessing to people who live or work in a built-up area like midtown Manhattan.

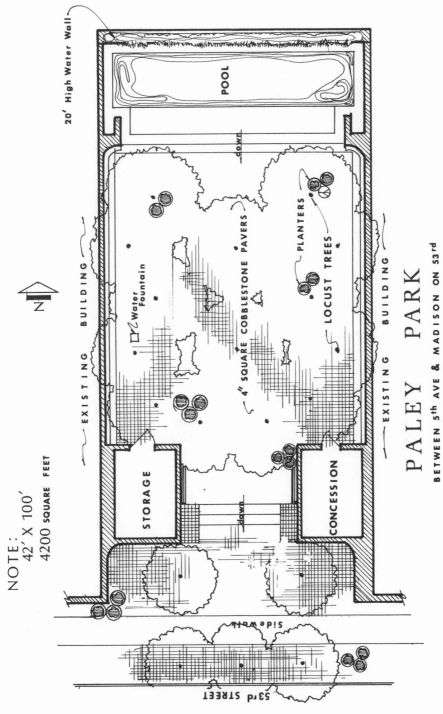

NOTE:
42' X 100'
4200 SQUARE FEET

N

20' High Water Wall

EXISTING BUILDING

POOL

down

Water Fountain

4" SQUARE COBBLESTONE PAVERS

PLANTERS

LOCUST TREES

EXISTING BUILDING

STORAGE

down

CONCESSION

Sidewalk

53rd STREET

PALEY PARK

BETWEEN 5th AVE & MADISON ON 53rd

NEW YORK CITY

SCALE $\frac{3}{32}$" = 1'–0"

FIG. 10

park itself, water falls down its face into a pool at the rate of thirteen hundred gallons per minute and is then recirculated. In place of the conventional park benches, there are individual chairs clustered around small tables topped with white marble. The entrance from the street has been narrowed to create two "gatehouses," at one of which coffee, soft drinks, and pastries are sold. The other contains mechanical equipment and storage facilities. The park opens to the public at 8 A.M. every day of the year; it is lighted after dark, and there is always an attendant on duty.

It is estimated that between two and three thousand people enjoy the calm of this mini-park every sunny day. Office workers eat their lunch at the foot of the waterfall; businessmen sit down to check over their papers; out-of-town visitors write letters home; white-haired oldsters neglect their needlepoint to chat with strangers; people of all ages rest and think their thoughts, relaxing while the world rumbles by. It is said that those who come to this park treat it as they would their own backyards. No attendant has ever had to ask a teenager twice to turn down his transistor radio, and, although the park stays open until 10 P.M. in pleasant weather (from May 1 to November 1), the police alarm system has never been used.

Paley is a pilot project that should inspire similar ventures. As William Paley said, "We should have more little parks in central urban locations. They would add greatly to the variety and delight of city life." His park works, and it shows that open space can be found even in the heart of a city and that it can provide an oasis.[3]

---

[3] Paley Park is administered by the William S. Paley Foundation, Inc., 51 W. 52d St., N.Y. Its designers were Zion and Breen Associates with A. Preston Moore, Architectural Consultant.

IX | The Suburbs: Case Studies

PRESERVING OPEN LAND in the suburbs is much like preserving it in urban areas, the difference being that economic and social pressures toward development are not so great. In places in the suburbs time still is operating on the side of conservation. Added to this is the fact that there are more options open for preservation, simply because there is more land available for various uses than in the city. In this chapter several case studies of suburban projects are examined for their open land implications.

TWO GREEN LEGACIES FOR DAYTONIANS

After World War II even in the suburbs and the countryside around Dayton, Ohio, the effects of urban sprawl were seen. Daytonians, like most Ohio residents, had long felt a closeness to nature, and most deplored the disappearance of open land in the city. But Dayton was caught up in the postwar growth and development. Fortunately, there were still places like the John W. Aull property near the city where the public was welcome to enjoy a bit of natural beauty. The Aull grounds, with their flowers, trees, and birds, were always delightful, but especially so in the spring and fall. When Mr. Aull died, his widow was faced with several choices. She could continue to live on the property and manage it and the adjoining farm, sell the land at a handsome price, or do something philanthropic. The idea of a place to help Daytonians maintain their strong feeling for nature—a nature center, and, perhaps later, an educational farm for youngsters—seemed to her to have real value.

Carl W. Buchheister, president of the National Audubon Society, encouraged Marie Aull's notion of a community nature center, and in 1956 she decided to fully endow such a center for the greater Dayton area. By giving most of her land (she retained tenancy of her home and its immediate grounds for life) and developing the necessary facilities, she established a prototype "land for learning" area. It was to be developed, owned, and operated by the National Audubon Society, a tax-exempt private organization which had set up similar centers in Greenwich, Connecticut, and El Monte, California.

The seventy-acre Aullwood Audubon Center was promptly established and opened to the public in 1957. To its gates came young and old. There, under the guidance of trained teacher-naturalists, schoolchildren are taught to be aware of the natural world about them and of their own responsibility in helping to maintain a healthy environment. The Center is also a wildlife sanctuary and features a wide variety of natural habitats—open fields and prairie, woodlands, spring-fed streams, ponds and marshes. A nature trail and guided trail tours lead visitors to the various areas. The natural vegetation provides a haven for foxes, raccoons, skunks, opossums, and many smaller mammals. Over fifty species of breeding birds have been recorded on the property. Fish, frogs, and turtles inhabit the freshwater areas. Spiders and insects abound, as do snails, centipedes, millipedes, and aquatic invertebrates.

A spacious nature interpretation building offers children and adults an opportunity to learn more about the outdoor world. Native live animals (except birds and mammals), seasonal exhibits, and "do-it-yourself" nature games make this a stimulating facility to visit. The building also houses classrooms, restrooms, a library, the service department, and administrative offices. School classes and youth groups of ten or more, from first grade through college, are invited to schedule a trip to the Audubon Center any time of the year. (Garden clubs and other adult groups may also schedule visits.) Each group, upon arrival, is briefed indoors prior to an outdoor trip. The outdoor walk, led by trained naturalists, is one of exploration, adventure, and learning. Back indoors, students can spend a few minutes in the exhibit room and service department. The group visit takes an hour and a half (two hours for sixth-grader and older groups, if desired). There is no charge. Both the Center and the Aullwood Farm (described below) work closely with local school systems to develop environmental teaching in all subjects at all grade levels. The Aullwood staff visits the schools, conducts field trips, and runs teacher workshops to develop awareness of ecology and to assist teachers in working their new knowledge into the existing curriculum. The refreshing thing about Aullwood is its simplicity. Facilities are adequate but not fancy. The emphasis is on outdoor learning and not indoor entertainment, and an optimal learning atmosphere prevails.

In 1963 Mrs. Aull decided to give her 120-acre working farm adjoining the Center to the National Audubon Society as an operating educational farm for the boys and girls of Dayton and its suburbs (see the photograph in Chapter II above). There are farm animals, equipment, buildings, croplands, and pastures, in addition to such natural features as woodlands, a duck pond, springs, and a stream. Trees in a maple woods are tapped for syrup each spring. An herb garden developed by a local garden club features plants used as medicines and condiments. Herbs are identified; identifications include braille signs for the blind. A century-old "bank barn" (with a built-on classroom) houses farm animals, hay, and equipment. Other buildings include the Thomas barn with a classroom, exhibits, and office space; a sheep shed; spring and sugar houses; a poultry house; and an herb house. Additional facilities include a windmill, bee hives, and a fruit orchard. One area of open land is being used by fifth-grade students as a school forest.

In the Old Farm Store visitors may purchase books, pictures, and charts relating to farm life and the out-of-doors, as well as honey, maple syrup, hand dipped candles, etc. The program offering at the Farm includes instruction in sound conservation principles, maintenance of fertile soil, production of high-yield crops, provision of cover, water, and natural food for wildlife habitats, raising of healthy animals for human consumption, and many other aspects of farm life. Equally important is the interpretation of farming as it affects the city dweller. Special weekend family programs are offered throughout the year: subjects are maple syrup, candle dipping, a Christmas program, sheep shearing, and honey harvest. Garden clubs and other adult groups may also schedule guided tours.

An endowment fund set up by Mrs. Aull covers all annual operating costs for the Farm and the Center except the salaries of two naturalists, paid by the Dayton Board of Education. Mrs. Aull also gave funds for all capital improvements. Taxes are paid by the Audubon Society on the land but not the buildings. (Tax exemption, however, varies greatly among different states.) These facilities and their programs are helping to develop a conservation conscience in Ohioans and others and are prototypes for other communities.[1]

NORTH HUDSON COUNTY PARK (Lower Palisades, N.J.)

Over seventy years ago quarrymen sliced away huge portions of the Hudson River Palisades and barged the traprock down to New York City to use in the construction of bridges, houses, office buildings, and sidewalks. Many years after the quarrying operation was forced up the river, the famous cliffs on the west side of the river, in New Jersey and New York State, became involved in a new fight for survival against a more subtle type of destruction, brought on by the slow but steady urbanizing of New Jersey.

Recently a plan to sell six acres of parkland in the area was announced. The tract is in the east corner of the 167-acre North Hudson Park in Hudson County. From it the visitor has a commanding view of the Manhattan skyline from the towers of Wall Street to the George Washington Bridge. The Hudson County Park Commission, appointed by the Board of Freeholders (the county governing board), transferred the "neglected" cliffside land to the Board to sell in March, 1969, with the idea that this area could generate new tax revenues. The sale was to be at public auction to the highest bidder at a minimum price of $200,000, and the buyer would have to agree to erect an apartment building at least thirty stories high.

When the plans to dispose of this parkland were announced publicly, a very strongly worded resolution was drawn up by the New York Regional Plan Association to stop the sale. It was signed by thirty-three conservation organizations and submitted to the Hudson County Board of Freeholders.[2]

---

[1] For further information write Aullwood Audubon Center, 1000 Aullwood Road, Dayton, Ohio 45414.

[2] The organizations were as follows: Anti-Pollution League; Appalachian Highlands Association; Bronx Council for Environmental Quality; Citizens Committee for the Hudson River; Citizens Committee for the Hudson Valley; Citizens Committee for the Protection of the Environment; The Conservation Center, Inc.; Essex County Natural Resources Committee; Federated Garden Clubs of New York, 10th District; Friends of the Hudson; the garden clubs of Morristown, Plainfield, Princeton, Short Hills, Somerset Hills, Stoney Brook, Summit, and Trenton; National Audubon Society National Campers and Hikers Association; New Jersey Audubon Society; New Jersey Division of the American Association of University Women; New Jersey Federation of Shade Tree Commissions; New Jersey Parks and Recreation Association; New Jersey Recreation and Parks Society; Open Space Institute; Palisades Historic Zoning Committee; Palisades Nature Association; Planning Association of North Westchester; Regional Plan Association; Road Review League; Sierra Club, Atlantic Chapter; and Sierra Club, Atlantic Chapter and North Jersey Group.

Albert W. Merck, of the well-known drug manufacturing family, chairman of the New Jersey Committee of the Regional Plan Association, denounced the sale in these terms: "A naturally wooded area could not possibly be unneeded in one of the most densely populated counties and with the least parkland per capita of any of the most urbanized counties in the most urban state in the nation. This parcel provides the public with a magnificent view of the river and skyline and a sense of openness. It is irreplaceable." He noted that the State of New Jersey, using funds provided by the Green Acres program, had approved acquisition of 470 acres of parkland in Hudson County over the last few years, of which 200 acres had already been acquired. "While the state invests, the county divests," Mr. Merck concluded.[3]

In a letter to John Keith, president of the New York Regional Plan Association, Richard J. Hughes, then Governor of New Jersey, stated:

> I have seen your letter regarding the prospective sale of six acres of parkland of the Lower Palisades in Hudson County.
>
> For your information, I have directed the Attorney General of New Jersey to join in suit to represent the public's interest in blocking the sale of this acreage. I have done this because our crowded State can ill afford to destroy what little open space is available to its citizens.
>
> In addition to joining in legal action, I have written the Secretary of the Interior requesting that his Department undertake a review of the proposed sale and comment on the merits of the proposal. I am hopeful that this information will be available to the public in order that the full facts of this sale might be made known.
>
> You may be assured that I will do everything within the limits of my authority to preserve this parkland in Hudson County.[4]

As the sale date drew near, Secretary of the Interior Walter J. Hickel threatened to cut off federal funds for parkland projects in Hudson County if the land were sold. He cited the fact that the county had been given $190,000 in matching funds for parks and recreation projects since 1965.

The public auction was suspended when Superior Court Judge John F. Lynch granted a restraining order asked in a suit against the sale filed by the Save the Palisades Association. After the pre-trial conference, Judge Lynch and representatives of both sides in the case visited the six-acre site. At the trial which followed, the judge granted a motion against the county, calling the proposal "an obviously transparent

---

[3] Quoted by Walter H. Waggoner in *New York Times*, May 13, 1969.
[4] Letter of June 9, 1969.

device aimed at circumventing legislative regulations." As Dudley B. Martin, a *New York Times* staff writer, summarized the problem: "The whole question rests on the observer's point of view. The race for ratables—taxes—is propelling the Palisades towns to permit cliffside developments as the demands for municipal services mount. But conservationists are prone to point out that, like Humpty Dumpty, the Palisades, once torn down, cannot be put together again."[5]

Quick, organized citizen action saved this part of the Palisades. As Richard Manly, the National Audubon Society representative at the hearings on the Palisades case, pointed out, "The difficulty with legal safeguards is that all, or very nearly all, legal covenants pertaining to land can be broken when the will to resist such pressures is lacking. Only when a community is aware of its open lands and waters and appreciates them can it be said that the integrity of parks and similar open lands is assured."[6]

KINGSPORT SAVES A MOUNTAIN

Bit by bit, most of the urban open land in Kingsport, Tennessee, had disappeared.[7] A new high school (built, ironically, without windows) had grabbed almost the last bit of precious greenery in the heart of town. In 1915, when Dr. John Nolen was planning the city, a 1,300-acre self-contained watershed was privately developed on neighboring Bays Mountain to supply the city's water. A dam was built and a pumping station installed, and a 45-acre reservoir was developed by 1916. The city bought the system in 1926. The water supply was adequate for two decades, but by 1944 the community had outgrown the capacity of the reservoir, and it was reclassified as a reserve water supply. Then the question arose of what to do with the mountain watershed area. Over the years many alternate uses were suggested. Most schemes involved selling the mountain and developing it. Fortunately, there were always some far-sighted aldermen who kept the city from selling the land. Today, thanks to those forgotten citizens, Kingsport has a wonderful mountain park preserve and nature center—and only six miles from the heart of downtown.

The events which led to Bays Mountain Park are comparatively recent.

5 *New York Times*, May 13, 1969.
6 Statement at public hearing, July 14, 1969, Courthouse, Jersey City, N.J.
7 This case study was prepared with the assistance of Dr. Merritt B. Shobe, chairman, Bays Mountain Parks Commission, Kingsport, Tenn.

In 1965 Mayor Rule appointed a committee to evaluate the watershed area for use as a city park. The committee, under the chairmanship of Alderman J. H. Lewis, a prominent businessman, recommended that the mountain, which was still essentially wild and undeveloped and accessible only to hikers and official vehicles, be set aside permanently as a mountain nature preserve. It also recommended that the area be opened to ordinary vehicular traffic but that development be restricted so as to maintain the tranquil natural atmosphere.

In 1966 some fifty interested citizens were brought together by Dr. Merritt B. Shobe, a local orthopedic surgeon, to discuss the possibility of taking steps to protect the mountain from commercial development. The group organized itself as The Friends of Bays Mountain. It created much interest among local civic clubs, was able to get publicity favorable to preserving the area, and created a positive climate of opinion in the community. The following year, Mr. Lewis, who had become Mayor, set up the Bays Mountain Park Commission, with Dr. Shobe as chairman, James C. White, past president of Tennessee Eastman Company, Karl Goerdell, James Thornton (who had recently done an independent study of the inadequate park and recreation facilities in and around the city), and Harry Steadman, an interested citizen and a contractor. The commission was instructed to create a park along the lines suggested in the Lewis report of 1965.

Before the appointment of the Commission, the Board of Mayor and Aldermen had made available for the park a legacy of approximately $150,000 which had been given to the city for park development in 1959 by the late Pearlie Wilcox, the first president of Tennessee Eastman Company. During the same period Tennessee Eastman, which had a private recreation area at the foot of the mountain, provided a major portion of a new park access road to the Bays Mountain area. Thus when the Commission began operations it had at its disposal 1,300 acres on the mountain, a 45-acre lake, a road to the top of the mountain, and sufficient funds for initial park planning.

The Commission began by drawing up a master plan for park development. The Nature Center Planning Division of the National Audubon Society was consulted and submitted a comprehensive plan. The Commission agreed to follow the Lewis committee recommendations and to adopt the Audubon plan without modification as the basis for park development. The basic idea was to create a nature education center of the highest quality. While the Audubon field survey was under way, it became evident that an adjoining watershed of 2,500 acres—a mountain area that comes to a natural point southwest of the existing park—would be needed to satisfy future demands on the park. Instead of using the Wilcox money for a nature center and other phases of park development, the Commission recommended that it be used to buy the additional land and that the financing of the nature center be worked out some other way. The Audubon planning team agreed that it was imperative to acquire the additional land before anything else was done. The Board of Mayor and Aldermen agreed.

Shortly thereafter, the city and the Commission were lucky enough to obtain a Bureau of Outdoor Recreation grant of $165,000. With this

FIG. 11

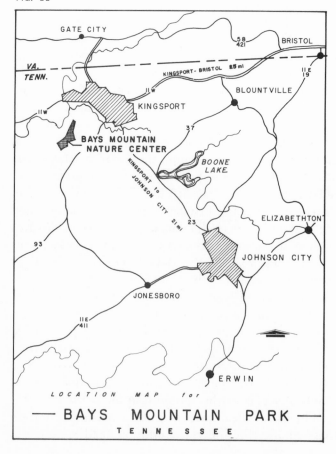

grant, matched by city funds and the balance of the Wilcox fund (some $30,000 of the fund had been spent on street improvements in another recreational area), the additional 2,500 acres were to be purchased. Since approval of the grant, approximately 1,500 acres of the area have been acquired by the city with its own and BOR funds.

The concept advanced was that the original Bays Mountain area be used for the nature preserve and nature center and that a part of the newly acquired land be established as a buffer zone, to be used only in ways compatible with the nature preserve idea. The lower portion of the new land, accessible by a different entrance road, could be devoted to the usual outdoor recreation uses.

In July, 1968, shortly after the Audubon report was presented, the Commission hired a park director, Robert F. Holmes, a forester-engineer, planner, and member of the Audubon team. Under his leadership the first phase of the plan was put into effect. A parking lot was constructed that summer, and in the fall the road to the main part of the park was improved, fire protection was initiated, an overlook and walkway were built on the dam, and a caretaker's residence was constructed. Late in the year telephone service and electric utilities were brought in (underground), and the next spring a water supply was provided.

In the fall of 1968 Arthur Stupka, a naturalist retired from the National Park Service (Great Smoky Mountains National Park) and former consultant to the Commission, began taking fifth- and sixth-graders from city and county schools on scheduled field trips. The next spring the Commission retained a local architect to design an interpretive building, and in August $225,000 was given by Tennessee Eastman for its construction. A special feature of the building is a planetarium with a forty-foot dome, approved in advance by city and county educators. The city also hired a chief naturalist, Jonathan West, former chief of interpretive services for the Pennsylvania state park system, to assist the park director. Construction of trails began in April, 1969, with the help of OEO funds. The spring of 1971 was the target date for opening the center for full-time use. Transportation will be available to the public by tram along the beautiful ridges and valleys within the nature center preserve.

The future integrity of Bays Mountain now seems assured. A stipulation of the Tennessee Eastman building gift was that the original 1,300 acres be permanently set aside by city ordinance as a park and nature preserve area. The 2,500 acres added would automatically be protected from development by the stipulations in the federal Bureau of Outdoor Recreation grant. It is anticipated that a permanent commission can be set up to operate the park within Kingsport's municipal framework. The Tennessee Valley Authority has been working with the park director on basic concepts for developing the limited-use buffer zone, the nature preserve, and the larger recreation area.

RESTON, VIRGINIA

Reston, in northeastern Virginia, is significant because of its open space aspects and its complete approach to planning. It is the first new town to be developed in accordance with the recommendations contained in the Washington, D.C., area Year 2000 Plan. The site is a slightly rolling, wooded, 6,800-acre tract in Fairfax County, approximately eighteen miles west of Washington, and four miles east of Dulles International Airport.

The Reston plan foresees a resident population of seventy-five thousand people by 1980, living in seven villages and other areas featuring a variety of buildings and dwellings—village centers, high-rise apartments, town houses, duplexes, and individual houses on large lots. High-density development is planned throughout the site rather than being concentrated in community centers. Town or village centers are planned to occupy a total of two hundred acres; selected light industry and government agencies are to occupy nine hundred acres. One village center and many dwelling units and individual homes have been built and occupied. A nature center is planned, and a beginning has been made in employing a naturalist to serve the new town.[8]

The chief attraction of Reston is its strong emphasis on open space and recreation. Residents can choose among different villages and housing areas built around certain forms of recreation, such as boating, golf, and horseback riding. Some 42 per cent of the site is planned for public use. The common open space is owned and maintained by a property owners' association.[9]

Reston offers walkways, footpaths, two lakes with a total area of a hundred acres, bridle paths, swimming, boating, fishing, and five golf courses. Plans call for a school, conference center, stores and other businesses, a museum, and a theater. The developer and planner have

---

[8] See survey and nature center plan for Reston, Virginia, prepared by the Nature Center Planning Division, National Audubon Society.

[9] "The Reston Story," Simon Enterprises, Fairfax, Virginia.

worked closely with county officials and religious groups to provide necessary schools and church facilities.

It was found that the density levels and open space planned for Reston could be achieved under the new community zoning district regulations (for planned residential areas) adopted by Fairfax County. Applicable to tracts in excess of 750 acres, the regulations fix a maximum population density of 11 persons per acre and, within this maximum, permits three types of residential density: high density, with 60 persons per gross residential acre; medium density, with 14 persons per gross residential acre; and low density, with 3.8 persons per gross residential acre.[10]

COLUMBIA, MARYLAND

Some seventeen miles southwest of Baltimore and twenty miles northeast of Washington, D.C., is the new city of Columbia, a privately planned hundred-million-dollar venture of the James W. Rouse Company of Baltimore. Begun in 1964 on fifteen thousand acres of rolling Maryland farmland, it is well under way. With a downtown center, village complexes, and varied business and dwelling units, the new city is an ambitious undertaking. The site is not as wooded as Reston's, as it was originally countryside, but in many respects the two concepts are similar. Columbia expects a versatile population of 110,000 people by 1980, many of whom will be working in the area. Duplexes, row houses, and multi-dwelling units are features which preserve a maximum amount of open space.[11]

---

[10] Gross residential acre is defined as density figured over an entire zoned area or subdivision.

[11] For further information write the Director of Information and Public Affairs, Rouse Company, Columbia, Md.

X | Some Regional Open Land Projects

EARLY IN THIS BOOK I spoke of population growth in the United States and the world and of the fact that most people today live in urban areas, a trend which is expected to increase. By 1980, according to Donald N. Michael, professor of psychology and program director for the University of Michigan Center for Research and Utilization of Scientific Knowledge, 80 per cent of the population of the United States will be living in urban areas, with especially heavy concentrations in a few regions.[1] There is already a New York, a Chicago, and a Los Angeles megalopolis, and Detroit, Washington, D.C., St. Louis, southern Florida, and San Francisco-Sacramento are also taking this shape. Open land planning in these regions seems imperative, although, as Professor Michael points out, we seem to be ill-prepared for it in knowledge and training. It seems appropriate at this point to look at some examples of what is being done on a regional basis in open land preservation, with the needs of people in great urban areas in mind. The case studies that follow are drawn from widely separated regions

[1] *The Unprepared Society* (New York: Basic Books, 1968), pp. 14–15.

and further differ from one another both in plan and in their basic approach to open land planning and preservation.

THE AMERICAN RIVER PROJECT

Sacramento County, which surrounds Sacramento, California, and also includes the city, is growing rapidly. In 1950 the population was 277,140; in 1960 the population was 502,778—an increase of 81.4 per cent—and the prediction is that by 1980 the population will be well over a million. During this period of population growth there has been no expansion in county size, which means that the amount of open space (parks and recreation areas) per person has been shrinking.

Through the middle of urban Sacramento flows the American River, bordered by miles of widely varied landscape, a large part of which is almost as it was in the Gold Rush a century ago. Because of its inaccessibility this lovely river with its almost unlimited recreation potential is virtually unknown to the majority of Sacramento County's new residents. The great majority of the population now has more leisure time, and this combined with availability of transportation and overcrowding of existing facilities, has challenged government agencies responsible for recreation and park services.

With the encouragement of various citizen's groups, the County Supervisors passed an ordinance establishing a County Department of Parks and Recreation and hired a competent professional director to advise the Board on an aggressive four-year program of land acquisition, design, development, programming, and construction of park and recreation areas and facilities, as well as advising and cooperating with officials of other local agencies. The Supervisors realized the political risk involved in expanding sizeable sums for a relatively long period without increasing public services, but the rising cost of land convinced those interested in the program that purchases would have to be made without delay.

Three regional park sites were selected on the fringe of the urbanized area, but most innovative was the concept of the American River Parkway. A citizen organization of particular influence, the Save the American River Association (SARA), dedicated itself to preserving the river and its natural areas. The group proposed a 5,000-acre greenbelt along twenty-three miles of flood plain from the confluence of the Sacramento and American rivers to Nimbus Dam, where it would merge with Folsom Lake State Park. The total protected area would con-

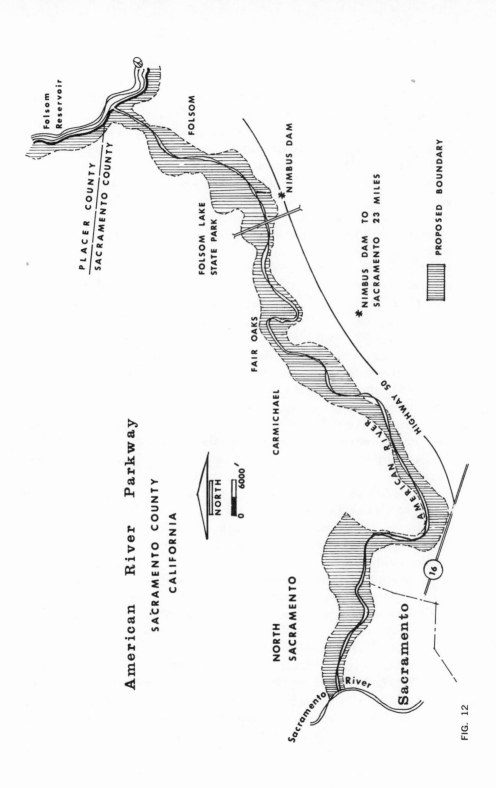

American River Parkway

SACRAMENTO COUNTY
CALIFORNIA

NORTH
SACRAMENTO

Sacramento

Sacramento River

AMERICAN RIVER

HIGHWAY 50

16

CARMICHAEL

FAIR OAKS

FOLSOM LAKE
STATE PARK

FOLSOM

NIMBUS DAM

PLACER COUNTY
SACRAMENTO COUNTY

Folsom Reservoir

NORTH

0   6000'

* NIMBUS DAM TO
SACRAMENTO 23 MILES

* NIMBUS DAM

PROPOSED BOUNDARY

FIG. 12

stitute 7,680 acres of recreation strip. After a number of public hearings the County Board of Supervisors officially adopted the proposal on January 24, 1962, as part of the general plan for Sacramento County.

Three regional parks have since then been developed in the Parkway, an eighteen-hole championship golf course was completed in 1964, some twenty miles of recreation trails are open, a fishing access point with boat ramp has been provided, and some nature areas have been protected. Today recreationists who are interested in rafts, kayaks, canoes, bank fishing, hiking, picnicking, and day camping are discovering the beauties of the American River. Moreover, the river is considered one of the best salmon and steelhead streams in California.

Other possible recreational facilities include boat marinas, picnic areas, overnight and day camping sites, livery stables, swimming, and field, target archery, outdoor rifle, pistol, and skeet ranges. Several sites are ideal for children's miniature farms, and model hydraulic mines, sluice boxes, water wheels, and other replicas of the days of the Forty-Niners would also be appropriate. A Huckleberry Finn or Tom Sawyer island could realistically transfer Mark Twain's stories of the Mississippi to Sacramento's local river.

Sacramento County controls approximately sixteen hundred acres of the American River Parkway. Approximately a thousand acres of land used for recreation is still owned by others, including the Boy Scouts, the Campfire Girls, a Park and Recreation District, and the State Fair Board. Through the Save the American River Association, thousands of citizens (including many children) purchased a certificate for "elbow room" at one dollar per square yard. The money was used to buy twelve acres of parkway land, the title of which now rests with Sacramento County. Such agreements as leases, easements, and licenses provide for public use of additional acreage.

To aid the acquisition program, the Housing and Home Finance Agency of the Federal Urban Renewal Administration (now a part of HUD) approved awards to Sacramento County totaling $501,569, which represented 30 per cent of the matching funds needed for open space lands. The development program has also been aided by the State of California Wildlife Conservation Board, which contributed $165,000 worth of fishing access facilities in the form of four-boat launching ramps at Discovery Park, at the western end of the Parkway. A unique major bridge, engineered to handle motor vehicles, pedestrians, and equestrians in a compatible manner, has been built with federal aid and state and county matching funds by the county Department of Public Works. In 1964 a $150 million bond measure for state parks and recreation helped in some types of open land recreation development. Many service clubs, fraternal groups, and individuals also donated equipment and labor to aid the Parkway. The Save the American River Association has recruited nearly four thousand life members dedicated to making the Parkway concept a reality. Through their efforts, a twenty-five-minute film called "Operation Star" and a half-hour documentary by a local television station have been produced, as well as a feature article in the October, 1964, issue of *Sunset Magazine*.

The American River case shows how community support can help to accomplish a task of great magnitude. The following rules seem to have been followed by the proponents of this successful project:

1. Think big and in regional terms. Try to develop community awareness and treat the problem as a regional one.
2. Take the lead in stressing the need for a comprehensive regional plan.
3. Assist all possible levels of government to develop the plan, but also set up a watchdog community organization to help oversee its execution.
4. Provide the framework for interested organizations and individuals to work together toward the common goal.
5. Help obtain the open lands required for public use in a fair and equitable manner.
6. Emphasize the need for quick and immediate action to acquire open lands before they are lost forever or priced out of the market for public purposes.
7. Follow the project through until completion; then continue high-quality maintenance and improvements.
8. Be constantly alert for threats to the integrity of the land and water areas that have been preserved.

THE WESTERN PENNSYLVANIA CONSERVANCY

One of the most notable private conservation groups working in the area of regional open land conservation is the Western Pennsylvania Conservancy. The organization began its work in the early 1930's when a group of citizens in western Pennsylvania, seeing their open spaces and natural areas disappearing, organized themselves as the Greater Pittsburgh Parks Association, a non-profit group. In 1951, when interest in urban and suburban parks had spread into the countryside, the Association changed its name to the Western Pennsylvania Conservancy. Today its eight thousand members concern themselves largely with park planning, land acquisition, and historic site preservation.

In its thirty years the Conservancy has rescued from development some thirty-five thousand acres of land ranging from nature preserves, park lands, and wildlife sanctuaries to historic landmarks. It has had special success in acquiring potential state park land. Unlike a government agency, it can move quickly to buy threatened areas and has done so on many occasions. After certain parcels of land are acquired, the acreage is turned over to the Division of Parks of the Commonwealth of Pennsylvania.The most significant such gifts to the state are McConnell's Mill State Park in Lawrence County, two thousand acres; Moraine State Park in Butler County, more than two thousand acres; Ohiopyle State Park in Payette County, ten thousand acres; Laurel Ridge State Park in Payette, Somerset, Westmoreland, and Cambria counties, eleven thousand acres; Oil Creek State Park in Crawford and Venango counties, nine hundred acres; Conemaugh George Scenic Area in Westmoreland and Indiana counties, twenty-five hundred acres. Other parkland purchases are in progress. The Conservancy is also credited with the acquisition of a number of significant natural areas, in addition to historical and architectural landmarks.[2]

THE MASSANUTTEN ADVENTURE

No one knows how the name Massanutten came about—Indians, some Virginians supposed. There was the mountain, rising sharply into the clouds, with fertile valleys all around, but those high mountain ridges were really a "mass of nuthin.' " Perhaps that's how Massanutten got its name. Today this vast mountain ecosystem is beginning to serve the hard-pressed residents of urbanizing Washington, D.C., an easy ninety-minute drive away.

The Massanutten development must be credited to one man, William (Big Bill) Huber, a Forest Service man who once headed the Smokey Bear program in Washington, D.C., and later became information-education chief for the southeastern region of the U.S. Forest Service in

[2] For further information write to the Western Pennsylvania Conservancy, 204 Fifth Avenue, Pittsburgh, Pa. 15222.

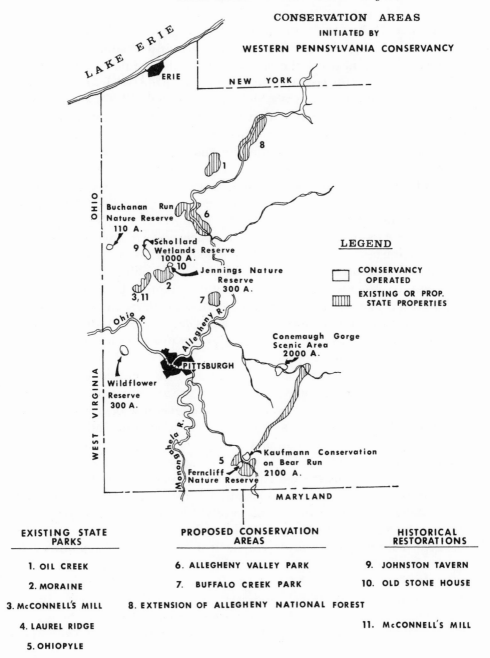

CONSERVATION AREAS
INITIATED BY
WESTERN PENNSYLVANIA CONSERVANCY

LAKE ERIE

ERIE

NEW YORK

OHIO

Buchanan Run
Nature Reserve
110 A.

Schollard
Wetlands Reserve
1000 A.

Jennings Nature
Reserve
300 A.

3, 11

2

7

Ohio R.

Allegheny R.

Conemaugh Gorge
Scenic Area
2000 A.

PITTSBURGH

Wildflower
Reserve
300 A.

WEST VIRGINIA

Monongahela R.

Kaufmann Conservation
on Bear Run
2100 A.

Ferncliff
Nature Reserve

MARYLAND

LEGEND

CONSERVANCY
OPERATED

EXISTING OR PROP.
STATE PROPERTIES

EXISTING STATE PARKS	PROPOSED CONSERVATION AREAS	HISTORICAL RESTORATIONS
1. OIL CREEK	6. ALLEGHENY VALLEY PARK	9. JOHNSTON TAVERN
2. MORAINE	7. BUFFALO CREEK PARK	10. OLD STONE HOUSE
3. McCONNELL'S MILL	8. EXTENSION OF ALLEGHENY NATIONAL FOREST	
4. LAUREL RIDGE		11. McCONNELL'S MILL
5. OHIOPYLE		

FIG. 13

Atlanta. Huber knew the million-acre George Washington National Forest in Virginia well. The Massanutten is a separate range in the forest in the heart of the Shenandoah Valley. Huber wondered why a great mountain ecosystem could not be made to serve five million northern Virginians and Washingtonians in some way—perhaps be used for outdoor interpretive education. John Baker, assistant to the Secretary of Agriculture at the time, was enthusiastic, as was Orville Freeman himself. The Washington and regional offices of the Forest Service told Huber to get a master plan worked out and to see what could be done. A private planning group was called in, a detailed survey was made, and a plan of action developed. The Forest Service had high praise for the plan and agreed to follow it.

The Massanutten Mountain comprehensive plan envisioned the site as one huge outdoor school which would offer general and specialized outdoor interpretive education programs to the public, both urban and rural. It proposed a specialized naturalist training program for Forest Service personnel, a resident outdoor school with facilities and environmental programs, including day camps for school children, facilities for clubs, and special outdoor features and programs for the physically and mentally handicapped.

The theme of the plan is nature appreciation and education. It showed that our basic need today is a deeper awareness and understanding of our environment, and Massanutten, because of its location, history, wildlife, plant life, and scenery, offered unique and ideal conditions for nature education on a large scale. The plan was to divide the mountain into three zones: a primary zone restricted to outdoor interpretation and conservation education; a secondary zone for scenic and non-consumptive outdoor recreational use (painting, photography, walking, etc.); and a third zone mostly devoted to outdoor recreation.[3] Because of the large area and the complex of institutional resources involved, three stages of development over a period of ten years were recommended.

In the first stage, to be completed within three years, the zoning and acquisition of additional land were to be carried out, and outdoor interpretive facilities and programs for school groups and the general public were to be initiated. The basic interpretive facility would be a

---

[3] For a review of the entire Massanutten plan, contact the U.S. Forest Service, Information-Education Branch, Atlanta, Ga. 30323. The plan was prepared by the Nature Center Planning Division, National Audubon Society.

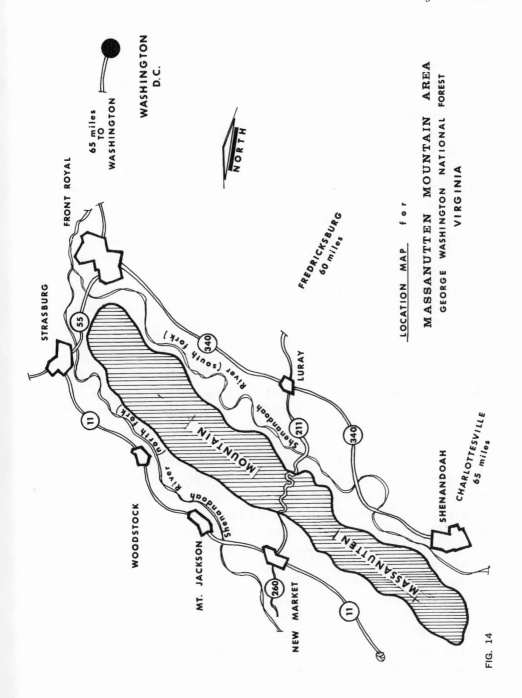

LOCATION MAP for

MASSANUTTEN MOUNTAIN AREA

GEORGE WASHINGTON NATIONAL FOREST

VIRGINIA

FIG. 14

nature center, set in an area of approximately five hundred acres, with an access road, parking lot, interpretive building, caretaker's residence, day-use school areas, and nature trails and trailside features. The spot chosen contained a stream, varied types of bottom land, an old home site, and slopes covered with numerous forest types. Its isolation and natural beauty provided a superb setting.

The second stage of development, over the next three years, would concentrate on the project headquarters, a center for in-residence trainees, an outdoor school, and a special education area. Headquarters were necessary in view of the size of the undertaking. The resident training center, an adult facility designed and established for the in-service training of forester-naturalists and other adults, seemed appropriate at this stage. The program of the outdoor school, a resident facility for fifth- and sixth-graders, would become an integral part of the curriculum of the school districts in the surrounding area. With the help of doctors and administrators from a local institution for the handicapped, a separate education area was planned, where the aged and the mentally and physically handicapped would find specially designed trails, shelters, rest areas, and instructional materials. The area would be open to the general public when not in use by special groups.

In stage three, the final four years of the plan, a number of historic sites were to be restored—iron smelting furnaces and the first Civilian Conservation Corps camp. A sportsmen's center, a tramway, lake, and a fenced, thousand-acre big-game reserve with buffalo and elk (once native to the area) were also to be added.

The comprehensive plan outlined was a big venture, with capital costs of over $5 million and annual operating costs of over $2.5 million, but the chances for a model outdoor interpretive education program on a suitable large parcel of national forest land had never seemed better. The groundwork has been laid, and public interest is increasing. Special trails and overlooks have been constructed, though cutbacks in federal spending in 1969 have delayed the program. Keen interest in the Massanutten project has been expressed by conservationists and educators from the Commonwealth of Virginia. The nearby counties and municipalities have offered their support, as have educators in the District of Columbia. With such strong federal, state, and local endorsement and financial support, the Massanutten undertaking may become one of the most successful such projects in the nation. The case study is significant not because a vast mountain region was preserved (it was already publicly owned) but because a large tract of land in the national forest system was made available for nature education to an expanding megalopolis. The project, though far from completion, has proved a milestone for the U.S. Forest Service.

AN UNDERWATER PARK EXPERIMENT

The first underseas park in the continental United States has become one of the largest and most unusual state parks in the nation. Covering 75,130 acres, most of which lies in the Atlantic Ocean off U.S. Highway 1 on Key Largo in the Florida Keys, the John Pennekamp Coral Reef State Park represents a special kind of land and water preservation. The Pennekamp reef is a combination of state and federal land holdings that have been preserved as a state park because they contain the only size- able living reef formations along the coast of North America. Other states have recognized the need for preserving their shorelines or coastal waters as well as their lands and are following Florida's lead in estab- lishing underwater state parks.

Pennekamp Park, some fifty-two miles south of Miami, contains forty of the fifty-two species of coral found in the Atlantic Reef system. Among them are such graphically named varieties as staghorn, moose- head, leaf, hat, finger, star, brain, flower, and cactus coral. This area is the spawning ground for rainbow-colored tropical fish, sport fish, sharks, barracudas, eels, turtles, and a wide assortment of other sea life. Skin and scuba divers come to Pennekamp from all over the world to explore its depths, while other visitors prefer to view the submarine spectacle from above the water. Weather permitting, glass-bottomed boats daily tour the reef area, where the incredible underwater marine and plant life can easily be seen through the clear water to a depth of sixty feet.

The park was named for John D. Pennekamp, a Miami newspaper editor long active in the conservation of natural properties in Florida. He is now a member of the Florida Park Board, served as legislative chairman of the state commission which created the famous Everglades National Park, and is the recipient of conservation awards from local, state, and national agencies for his work in Florida. Pennekamp Park was created mainly because commercial shell, coral, and fish collectors were destroying the area's natural values. Now protected by the Park

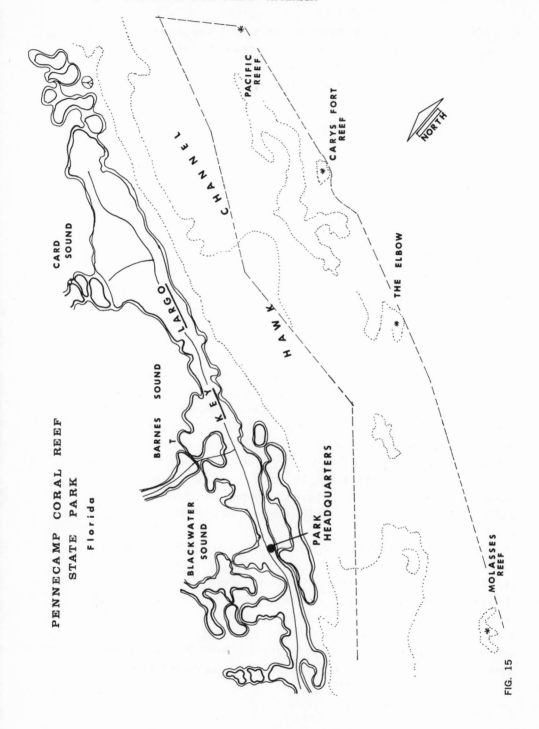

PENNECAMP CORAL REEF
STATE PARK
Florida

CARD SOUND

CHANNEL

KEY LARGO

BARNES SOUND

BLACKWATER SOUND

PARK HEADQUARTERS

PACIFIC REEF

CARYS FORT REEF

THE ELBOW

HAWK CHANNEL

MOLASSES REEF

NORTH

FIG. 15

Board, the area cannot be tampered with by treasure hunters, curio collectors, or vandals. The submarine growths are thus safe from spear-fishing or poaching.

After acquisition of the submerged area from state and federal sources, the above-water land of the park on Key Largo was acquired largely through two anonymous gifts from a Miami Beach family. First opened in 1963, the park offers the visitor every variety of water sport, including swimming, fishing, boating, waterskiing, skin and scuba diving, and underwater photography. The land area contains a marina that is complete with boat dock. The focal point of the reef is the "Christ of the Deep," a nine-foot bronze statue, a gift from Italy, that was placed beneath the water to symbolize peace. Pennekamp Park is a notable example of the preservation of underwater lands and life. Most significant of all, as Alexander Sprunt IV, National Audubon Society biologist, puts it, the park "preserves a major and unique marine ecosystem in the highly vulnerable Florida Keys."

ROOKERY BAY

It seems apparent that if open land, including water, is to remain a part of the urban landscape, the various interest groups most concerned must be brought together. Those seeking to develop land areas and those seeking their protection and non-use can arrive at some kind of a workable solution if both bargain in good faith. An outstanding example of an attempt by private developers and conservationists to cooperate in providing for an expanded urban community and at the same time protecting a vital natural environment is the case of Rookery Bay in southern Florida.

Rookery Bay is a complex of land and water halfway between Naples, Florida, and Marco Island. It contains a 4,000-acre wildlife sanctuary now owned and managed by the National Audubon Society. It is, as Jack Allen, the sanctuary manager, says, "a fountain of the great Ten Thousand Islands region in South Florida" that dips into the Gulf of Mexico. The area is rich in plants and animals and is a spawning and rearing ground for fish, shellfish, and other marine organisms. Geologically and historically the region is unique. From a developers' standpoint, the land and water resources, because of the proximity of Naples (a small Gold Coast city), the Gulf of Mexico, the Ten Thousand Islands, and the Everglades National Park, is very tempting. The question is whether development and conservation can work together

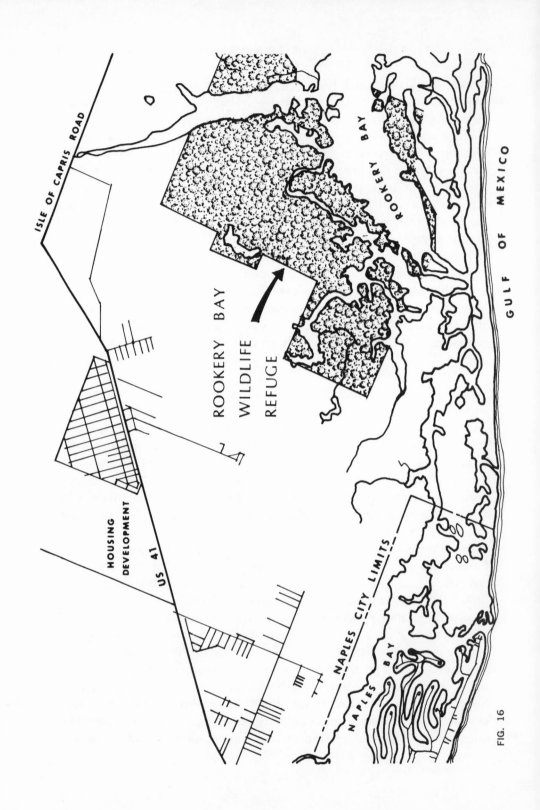

ISLE OF CAPRIS ROAD

ROOKERY BAY

GULF OF MEXICO

ROOKERY BAY
WILDLIFE
REFUGE

HOUSING
DEVELOPMENT

US 41

NAPLES CITY LIMITS

NAPLES BAY

FIG. 16

to create an environment suitable both to man and other living forms of life—whether a region like this can be developed as a satellite urban area and still keep its natural values.

The story begins in the early 1960's, when the National Audubon Society, with the help of many groups, began to acquire parcels of land around the bay as a strategic natural environment. Soon a race with the bulldozer began. Both new and older Naples residents have a deep appreciation of their natural surroundings, and Naples became nationally known as the town that put up the fight of its life for the environment. In 1964 the Collier County Conservancy was born. The battleground was clear—Rookery Bay, an estuary of six square miles containing a maze of islands and feeder streams. The conservation forces were the Nature Conservancy, the National Audubon Society, a host of local and Florida organizations, and fifteen hundred militant citizens.

A cross-section of the community, ranging from school children to the very wealthy, soon joined together and began a fund drive. A total of $300,000 was raised to help save the area and was matched by $150,000 from the National Audubon Society. With this money 2,600 acres of land and 1,400 acres of state-owned waters were purchased, and the first effort to retain coastal open space north of Everglades National Park was under way. Not one cent of state or federal funds was asked for or received. The significance of the response, really a mandate from the community, transcends the establishment of a wildlife sanctuary and indicates that environmental poverty is no longer to be ignored or tolerated in this region. The wildlife sanctuary of 4,000 acres was established and has passed into the hands of the National Audubon Society.

Several waves of culture have passed over the Rookery Bay area in the past two thousand years. Calusa Indians and Spaniards came and went, leaving scarcely a trace of their presence. Seminole Indians wisely adapted their ways to those of the land and waters. The impact of the past twenty-five years by far overshadows that of all other forces at work since this area, a peninsula, arose from the sea fifty million years ago. It is ironic that the climate, subtropical vegetation, wildlife, islands, and waterways proved so attractive that man has almost destroyed them in his quest to enjoy them. Shallow bays and mangrove shorelines, keys to survival for marine life and man alike, are most vulnerable. Because of the ease and profitability of transforming marshes, islands, and waterways into glistening villa-studded subdivisions and commercial enterprises, these natural treasures are in jeopardy. Rookery Bay Wildlife Sanctuary is an opening salvo in the battle for preservation of the entire Ten Thousand Islands region.

A long, narrow barrier island lies between Rookery Bay and the Gulf of Mexico. Covered with tropical hammock vegetation, this shield is a prime factor in protecting the sanctuary's mangrove forest. About one third of the acreage of the sanctuary consists of saltwater creeks and bays. Another third is tidal overflow mangrove forest. The remainder consists of sand ridges and shell mounds. Tamiami limestone bedrock emerges at the landward boundary and slopes to a depth of fifteen feet beneath the surface at the coast. Between these extremes are soils composed of sand, marl, and red mangrove peat. Mangrove forest occupies most of the islands and waterways. Upland is characterized by small brackish ponds, prairies, and rock outcrops. Higher land is marked by stands of pine, palmettos, and cabbage palms. Solution holes through soft bedrock create a desert-like habitat adjacent to marshland, and cacti often flourish within a few feet of aquatic plants.

Rookery Bay is a modified marine environment, an extension of the Gulf of Mexico rather than an estuary dependent solely upon nutrients from uplands. Mangroves produce basic plant material but may be more important as huge nutrient traps. Organic material is filtered from tidal surges, broken down by microorganisms, and carried through the estuary, thus renewing the cycle. Open waters support maximum phytoplankton populations, while sea grasses and other higher aquatic plants provide prime nursery and feeding grounds for marine life and water birds. The American oyster has long been a prominent animal here, as attested by the many shell mounds formed by Indians and by natural deposits. Oysters and most of the invertebrates are filter feeders dependent upon planktonic organisms.

Wildlife is abundant at Rookery Bay. Pelicans, cormorants, and wading birds play a vital role in the water cycles of life. Through crustaceans and fishes manurial salts stimulate growth of the food chain base terminating with man. Upland mammals include deer, raccoon, bobcat, and black bear, while porpoise and manatee ply the warm and shallow waters. Brackish ponds and uplands provide breeding and feeding grounds for the bald eagle, fulvous tree duck, mangrove cuckoo, and other wildlife. The Rookery Bay Wildlife Sanctuary is thus of great importance to sport and commercial fisheries, since almost all saltwater fish and shellfish are dependent upon estuaries during a portion of their life cycle. "Even more important," according to John Anderson, director of the Sanctuary Department of the National Audubon Society, "Rookery Bay and other red mangrove forests are the key to the healthy ecology of the whole region."

Rare indeed are those who appreciate the delicate relationships between mingling fresh and salt water, sea grasses, shrimp, manatees, and herons. Yet fifteen hundred people raised a united voice to protect this unique complex. When asked about the source of their interest, their answers could be boiled down to something like "I just like to know that there will still be some green, quiet and uncluttered places left nearby." This was the feeling of boaters, fishermen, birders, and just "lookers." No one said "I don't want Florida to look like Big Town with sunshine," but the specter of neon lights, parks festooned with cans and melon rinds, and water saturated by pollutants loomed ominously. Land values surrounding the Sanctuary have risen tenfold since its acquisition in 1966.

It is presumptuous, Jack Allen, the sanctuary manager, says, to assume that man can improve upon an intricate ecological complex. An ultimate management scheme would prohibit any activity including those related to wildlife management, which would alter a single organism. Unfortunately, such a program is not possible. Much of the fifteen thousand acres surrounding the sanctuary is in large holdings, with two-thirds owned by six corporations and individuals. Thus the dual objectives of safeguarding the sanctuary and of high-quality development were the focus of concern. A team of engineers, ecologists, botanists, marine biologists, and planners were assembled by the Conservation Foundation in Washington, D.C. A preliminary six-month investigation was conducted in 1968 and 1969, and the resultant development concept outlined procedures which might accomplish these dual objectives. The basic recommendations include:

1. creation of a single association of landowners through which private land development can be integrated under a comprehensive plan;
2. pollution control safeguards, including central water and sewage systems serving the entire drainage area; protection from sedimentation generated by dredging and land clearing operations; control of runoff of fertilizers and pesticides;

3. retention of the balance of fresh water runoff entering the system during the rainy season to prevent rapid drops in salinity levels;
4. use of planning and design techniques such as cluster and open space communities to help minimize environmental deterioration;
5. limitation of access to islands within the project area for recreational purposes to boats, as bridges, roads, and parking areas take up acreage and destroy scenic values.

The potential pollutants referred to in the development plan are all water-borne and include domestic sewage, pesticides, and agricultural fertilizers and wastes. An adequate sewage system, upland settling basins, and pesticide controls can solve these problems. More subtle and perhaps more detrimental may be "people-pollution". Planners have proposed a network of a hundred miles of perimeter and lateral canals within the development area. Waterways dredged through existing soils, sand and marl, are subject to devastating erosion. Although three enforcement agencies attempt to control pollution and wake damage caused by boats in Naples Bay, it continues unabated. The only effective control of wake erosion now available is installation of concrete bulkheads. Are greenbelt and open space concepts compatible with concrete waterways? Channels would have to be dredged through Rookery Bay and its primary feeder stream, Henderson Creek, to permit access to residential waterways. Soil borings taken in the bay indicate that boat traffic, although now minimal because of shallow depths, has already obliterated many of the islands and is eroding the shoreline. The question arises of whether channels and waterways can be justified solely on the basis of the economics of development.

Solution of some seemingly minor problems associated with human inhabitation may require specialized engineering techniques as yet untested. Lawns surrounding the proposed sixteen thousand homes will consist of sod grown elsewhere and placed over sand, shell, and marl fill. Summer rains leach nutrients from the sod into waterways, through which they proceed to their terminus, Rookery Bay. One average lot requires a minimum of six hundred pounds of fertilizer per annum; thus an additional four thousand tons of nutrients would be deposited in Rookery Bay from residential areas alone each year. Waters of this basin support one of the highest plankton populations in Florida, and the line between high productivity and organic pollution is indeed a fine one. The "plankton explosion" could cause repeated and prolonged oxygen depletions resulting in extensive destruction of fish, shellfish, and other marine animals. This artificially induced broth would be quite similar to the dread "red tide" which periodically decimates animal life in the Gulf. Before the development concept can be transformed into a working plan, intensive hydrological and engineering studies must be made. A newly established marine laboratory on Shell Island, within the sanctuary, has begun the hydrological work. A grant from the U.S. Department of the Interior, Office of Water Resources Research, enabled the University of Miami Institute of Marine Sciences to initiate its own investigations in January 1970.

Surprisingly, there is some reason for optimism that at least some of the problems associated with this enormously complicated venture can be resolved. If conservationists and developers sit down and try to work things out, it may be possible to demonstrate that bulldozer and dragline can be used constructively to provide environmental quality for people—and perhaps save a large natural region. Meanwhile, wildlife biologists and ecologists, although cautiously optimistic, are also apprehensive. As Alexander Sprunt points out, "We are talking here about the very survival of a major plant and animal environment. If it goes, what about the Everglades National Park, the rest of tropical Florida, and . . . man?"

Appendixes

Appendix 1

The Natural Lands Trust, Philadelphia

Charter and Articles of Incorporation

CHARTER OF NATURAL LANDS TRUST, INCORPORATED

In the Court of Common Pleas of Philadelphia County
In Re Incorporation   :
      of   :
                                :

NATURAL LANDS TRUST, INCORPORATED :

Articles of Incorporation
of
NATURAL LANDS TRUST, INCORPORATED

To the Honorable, the Judges of the Said Court:

The undersigned, all of whom are citizens of the United States and of full age and at least three of whom are residents of the Commonwealth of Pennsylvania, desire to form a nonprofit corporation under the Nonprofit Corporation Law (Act of May 5, 1933, P. L. 289 as amended) and to that end do hereby state:

1. *Name*: The name of the proposed corporation is Natural Lands Trust, Incorporated. This name has been registered with the Department of State within six months of the date of this application, and a certificate of registration is attached.

2. *Registered Office*: The proposed corporation's initial registered office in this Commonwealth will be at Room No. 1308, 1500 Walnut Street, Philadelphia 2, Pennsylvania.

3. *Purpose*: The purpose of the proposed corporation is to preserve lands, waters and wildlife in their natural state and to broaden the opportunities for public enjoyment of natural areas by:

    a. Providing a convenient medium through which anyone may make gifts—whether of land, securities, cash, or any other kind of property—in furtherance of conservation;

    b. Acquiring and preserving, and helping others to acquire and preserve, all kinds of natural areas—such as, for example, woods, fields, streams, marshes, seashore, and other open spaces—located within the United States of America or any of its possessions; and

    c. Making these areas available to the public under such conditions as will preserve their natural state and at the same time enable present and future generations to use them for appropriate recreation, enjoyment, and education.

4. *No Profit for Members*: The proposed corporation does not contemplate pecuniary gain or profit, incidental or otherwise, to its members.

5. *Term of Existence*: The term of the proposed corporation is to be perpetual.

6. *Incorporators*: The names and places of residence of the incorporators are:

Name	*Residence*
Sanford D. Beecher	209 Rhyl Lane Cynwyd, Pa.
Charles J. Biddle	Andalusia, Pa.
George R. Clark	W. Valley Green Road Flourtown, Pa.
Emily T. duPont	Greenville, Delaware
Allston Jenkins	1799 E. Willowgrove Avenue Philadelphia 18, Pa.
Herbert H. Mills	Bridgeton, New Jersey
Erard A. Matthiessen	River Bank Road Stamford, Conn.

7. *Directors*: The names and places of residence of the persons who are to act as directors under the election of their successors are:

Name	*Residence*
Sanford D. Beecher	209 Rhyl Lane Cynwyd, Pa.
Charles J. Biddle	Andalusia, Pa.
George R. Clark	W. Valley Green Road Flourtown, Pa.

Emily T. duPont   Greenville, Delaware
Allston Jenkins   1799 E. Willowgrove Avenue
                              Philadelphia 18, Pa.
Herbert H. Mills   Bridgeton, New Jersey
Erard A. Matthiessen   River Bank Road
                              Stamford, Conn.

8. *Members*: The persons serving from time to time as directors of the proposed corporation shall be its only members.

9. *No Stock*: The proposed corporation is to be organized on a non-stock basis.

10. *Tax Exemption*: The proposed corporation shall always be so operated that:

> a. As long as the federal income-tax, estate-tax, and gift-tax laws allow an exemption or deduction for gifts for charitable, scientific, or educational purposes, gifts to the proposed corporation will qualify for that exemption or deduction.

Signed   , 1961.

_____ (SEAL)
SANFORD D. BEECHER

_____ (SEAL)
GEORGE R. CLARK

_____ (SEAL)
ALLSTON JENKINS

_____ (SEAL)
HERBERT H. MILLS

_____ (SEAL)
CHARLES J. BIDDLE

_____ (SEAL)
EMILY T. DUPONT

_____ (SEAL)
ERARD A. MATTHIESSEN

COMMONWEALTH OF PENNSYLVANIA:
                                  SS
COUNTY OF PHILADELPHIA   :

Before me a Notary Public in and for the County aforesaid personally came Sanford D. Beecher, Allston Jenkins and Charles J. Biddle, three of the above named Incorporators who in due form of law acknowledged the foregoing instrument to be their act and deed for the purposes therein specified.

SANFORD D. BEECHER

ALLSTON JENKINS

CHARLES J. BIDDLE

Witness my hand and seal of office the   day of
1961.

Notary Public

Joseph A. Birchill, Notary Public
Philadelphia, Philadelphia County
My Commission expires February 1, 1965

IN THE COURT OF COMMON PLEAS
OF PHILADELPHIA COUNTY

In Re:	C. P. No. 6
Application for Charter	December Term, 1960
of Natural Lands Trust	
Incorporated	No. 3511

DECREE

And now, this   day of   , A.D., 1961, an
application for charter for Natural Lands Trust, Incorporated under the
provisions of the "Nonprofit Corporation Law", approved May 5, 1933, as
amended, having been presented for approval to me, a law judge of the
said County, together with the Articles of Incorporation, proof of advertising and the Certificate of the Department of State pertaining to the registration of the corporate name, I do hereby certify that I have perused and
examined the said instruments and that I find them to be in proper form
and within the provisions and requirements of said Act, the purposes given
in the articles to be lawful and not injurious to the community and the
proposed name presently available for corporate use.

It is, therefore, ordered and decreed that the Articles of
Incorporation of the Natural Lands Trust, Incorporated be and the same
are hereby approved and upon the recording of the said Articles of Incorporation and this decree, the corporation shall come into existence for the
purposes and upon the terms stated therein.

WITNESS my hand and seal of the said Court.

Judge

Declaration of Trust
establishing
THE NATURAL LANDS TRUST
*****

Girard Trust Corn Exchange Bank (hereinafter called the trustee), of Philadelphia, Pennsylvania, hereby declares that it will receive and hold property in trust as follows:

1. *Title*: This trust shall be known as "The Natural Lands Trust".
2. *Duration*: This trust shall exist perpetually.
3. *Purpose*: The purpose of this trust is to provide a convenient medium through which anyone may make gifts—whether of land, securities, cash, or any other kind of property—for the support of the work of Natural Lands Trust, Inc., a Pennsylvania nonprofit corporation.
4. *Contributors*: Any person, trust, corporation, or other form of organization may make gifts of any kind to this trust.
5. *Trustee's Functions*: The trustee's primary functions shall be to receive gifts to this trust and allocate them to the principal of it, to keep the principal and any surplus income invested to such extent as may be appropriate, and from time to time to remit funds to Natural Lands Trust, Inc., for application by it towards its corporate purposes. All remittances shall be made on requisitions authorized by the Board of Directors of Natural Lands Trust, Inc.
6. *Income Remittances*: There shall be no limit on the amount of income the trustee may remit to Natural Lands Trust, Inc.
7. *Principal Remittances*: Remittances of principal to Natural Lands Trust, Inc., shall be limited as follows:
   a. Principal may be remitted solely for the purpose of enabling Natural Lands Trust, Inc., to acquire natural areas—such as, for example, woods, fields, streams, marshes, seashore, and other open spaces—or to meet capital expenses incident to natural areas already held by it; and
   b. The aggregate amount of all principal remitted from time to time shall never exceed one-third of the aggregate original value of all gifts to this trust cumulated from the date of its creation.
8. *Trustee's Investment Powers, etc.*: The trustee shall have full authority:
   a. To invest in and to retain all kinds of real or personal property, whether or not it is productive of income, without regard to any limitations imposed by law on investments by trustees;
   b. To hold property unregistered or in the name of a nominee;
   c. To give proxies, both ministerial and discretionary;
   d. To compromise claims;
   e. To join in any merger, reorganization, voting-trust plan, or other

concerted action of security holders, and to delegate discretionary duties with respect thereto;

f. To sell at public or private sale, to exchange, or to lease for any period of time, any real or personal property, and to give options for sales or leases; and

g. To allocate any property received or charge incurred to principal or income, or partly to each, without being obliged to apply the usual rules of trust accounting.

These authorities shall be exercisable without approval of any court or of Natural Lands Trust, Inc.

9. *Substitution*: If Natural Lands Trust, Inc., should ever fail to qualify as a tax-exempt organization under the federal income-tax laws or if it should ever cease to exist, thereupon the trustee shall select another organization that has similar objectives and in addition is tax-exempt, and thereafter the organization so chosen shall succeed to all rights of Natural Lands Trust, Inc., in the income and principal of this trust. Similar substitutions shall be made as often as may be needed to meet the requirements of Paragraph 10 hereof.

10. *Tax Exemption*: This trust shall always be so operated that:

a. As long as the federal income-tax laws allow an exemption for trusts organized and operated exclusively for charitable, scientific, or educational purposes, this trust will qualify for that exemption; and

b. As long as the federal income-tax, estate-tax, and gift-tax laws allow an exemption or deduction for gifts for charitable, scientific, or educational purposes, gifts to this trust will qualify for that exemption or deduction.

11. *Irrevocability*: This declaration may be altered to this extent:

a. If one or more similar trusts should be established for the support of the work of Natural Lands Trust, Inc., the trustee may change the name of this trust so as to distinguish it from the others; and

b. The trustee may from time to time alter the terms of this declaration to such extent, if any, as may be necessary or appropriate to qualify this trust as a tax-exempt organization under the federal income-tax, gift-tax, and estate-tax laws in force from time to time.

Otherwise this declaration, and the trust created by it, shall be irrevocable and unalterable.

12. *Trustee's Compensation*: The trustee's compensation shall be calculated conformably to the standard schedule of rates established from time to time by the Board of Directors of Girard Trust Corn Exchange Bank and shall be charged against the income of this trust.

In Witness Whereof Girard Trust Corn Exchange Bank has caused this instrument to be executed this   day of   1960.

GIRARD TRUST CORN EXCHANGE BANK

By:_____

President

Attest:_____

Secretary

COMMONWEALTH OF PENNSYLVANIA :

: SS

COUNTY OF PHILADELPHIA   :

On this, the   day of   A.D. 1960, before me, the undersigned officer, personally appeared   , who acknowledged
himself to be the   of Girard Trust Corn Exchange Bank,
and that he as such   being authorized so to do, executed the
foregoing instrument for the purpose therein contained by signing the name
of the Girard Trust Corn Exchange Bank by himself as
In Witness Whereof I have hereunto set my hand and official seal.

_____

Notary Public

Appendix 2

Scenic Easement Protecting Mount Vernon

Deed

THIS DEED, made this   day of   19 ,
by and between
parties of the first part, and the United States of America, party of the
second part.

WITNESSETH:

WHEREAS, the Act of October 4, 1961 (Public Law 87-362),
enacted for the preservation and protection of certain lands in Prince
Georges and Charles Counties, Maryland, and for other purposes, authorizes
the Secretary of the Interior to acquire scenic easements by donation or
other appropriate means and to enter into agreements and covenants with
property owners and others for the preservation of the scenic values of the
area described in the said Act; and

WHEREAS, the parties of the first part are the owners in
fee of certain real property, hereinafter described, situate in
County, Maryland, included within the area covered by the said Act of
October 4, 1961, and over which the Secretary of the Interior has determined it to be necessary to acquire a scenic easement in order to assure
uniform application of scenic control over the area covered by the said Act
of October 4, 1961;

NOW, THEREFORE, for and in consideration of the
foregoing and of the desire of the parties of the first part to assure preservation of their lands and of others in the vicinity affecting their lands, the
parties of the first part, do hereby grant and convey, in perpetuity, subject
to the conditions hereinafter set forth, unto the United States of America
and its assigns an estate, interest, and scenic easement in said real property

146

of the parties of the first part, of the nature and character and to the extent hereinafter expressed to be and to constitute a servitude upon said real property of the parties of the first part, and to that end and for the purpose of accomplishing the intent of the parties hereto, said parties of the first part covenant on behalf of themselves, their heirs, successors, and assigns, with the United States of America and its assigns to do and refrain from doing, severally and collectively, upon the said lands of the parties of the first part, the various acts hereinafter mentioned, it being hereby agreed and expressed that the doing and the refraining from said acts, and each thereof, upon said lands are and will be for the benefit of the United States of America through the preservation for the benefit of present and future generations of the historic and scenic values of lands comprising the principal overview from Mount Vernon and from Fort Washington, in accordance with the said Act of October 4, 1961.

The restrictions hereby imposed upon the use of said lands of the parties of the first part, and the acts which said parties of the first part so covenant to do and refrain from doing upon their said lands in connection therewith, are and shall be as follows:

1. The lands shall not be used for any professional or commercial activities except such as can be and are in fact conducted from a residential dwelling without alteration of the dwelling.

2. No trailer shall be used on the lands as a substitute for a residential building or other structure except on a temporary basis, not to exceed one year.

3. The lands shall not be used as a site for any of the following: airports, hotels, taverns, dance halls, apartment houses, flats, boarding houses, cemeteries, schools, nurseries, golf courses, hospitals, churches, sand, gravel, or clay pits, sawmills, skeet or golf driving ranges, commercial swimming pools, tourist homes or cabins, trailer camps, entertainment centers, dumps, junk yards, greenhouses not attached to dwellings. Nothing here, however, shall be deemed to prohibit the use of residential dwellings for purposes which can be and are in fact conducted therein without alteration of the dwelling.

4. The land shall not be used as a site for any major public utilities installations such as electric generating plants, electric power substations, high tension electric power transmission lines, gas generating plants, gas storage tanks, water storage tanks or reservoirs, sewage treatment plants, microwave relay stations, or telephone exchanges. Nothing herein shall, however, be deemed to prevent the construction or maintenance on, over, or under the lands of facilities usual to a residential neighborhood such as telephone and electric lines and water mains.

5. No advertising signs or billboards shall be displayed or placed upon the land, with the exception of professional name plates and signs not larger than two square feet advertising home occupations or products or the sale or lease of the lands.

6. No mining or industrial activity shall be conducted on the lands.

7. No part of any of the lands is to be sold or leased in lots smaller than five acres.

8. No building shall be erected, altered, placed or permitted to be built or remain on the said lands, except that on each five-acre parcel thereof there is permitted to be one detached single dwelling and such guest house, garage, stable or other outbuildings which may be required for the need of the owner or occupant of such residence. In the event the lands described in this instrument are less than five acres in area, the provisions of the preceding sentence shall apply as if the land were exactly five acres in area. In no case is any building to be constructed on the lands described herein which, when completed, is to be used for any of the purposes which are expressly prohibited in this instrument.

9. No tree larger than six inches in diameter and thirty feet in height shall be cut down without the written permission of the Secretary of the Interior or his authorized representative.

Plans for the removal of trees for the clearing of homesites shall be submitted to the Secretary of the Interior or his designated representative for approval. In passing upon such plans the said Secretary or his designated representative shall take into consideration not only the needs of the landowner but also the extent of clearing around similar homesites in the vicinity.

Permission need not be obtained for the removal of trees by or upon advice of the appropriate utility company or other organization for the purpose of protecting utility lines or water or sewer mains. Likewise, permission need not be obtained for the removal of dead, diseased, or injured trees when such removal is necessary for reasons of safety.

10. Approval of a requested action shall be deemed to have been granted if the Secretary of the Interior or his designated representative has not responded to a written request within thirty days.

11. No dump of ashes, trash or any unsightly offensive material shall be placed upon the land, except that in eroding areas of a drainage system where surface water runoff is destroying the natural ground cover, suitable heavy fill may be so placed as to control and prevent further erosion provided said fill is covered by arable soil or humus.

It is understood and agreed that the imposition of the covenants and restrictions set forth herein are in no way intended to nullify, supersede, or amend any covenants or restrictions which have heretofore or which may hereafter be placed upon said lands.

The lands of the parties of the first part, hereinabove referred to and to which the provisions of this instrument apply, are situated in the County of   , State of Maryland, and are more particularly described as follows [the description follows].

Nothing herein shall be deemed to affect any mortgage, lien, or other interest in the lands described herein which was in existence at the time of the recordation of this instrument in the county land records.

It is understood and agreed that the parties of the first part or their successors in interest to the lands described herein shall not be required to pay an admission fee to the park area authorized by the aforesaid act of October 4, 1961.

The easement and rights herein granted shall forthwith terminate and be of no further force and effect should any one or more of the following events occur and should the parties of the first part or their successors in interests to the land described herein register with the Secretary of the Interior a notice in writing that they no longer desire to have the lands described herein encumbered by the easement and rights herein contained:

(a) Should the United States fail to obtain scenic easements over a substantial proportion of the tracts in the area described in section 2(c) of the aforesaid act of October 4, 1961, within five years from the date of this deed;

(b) Should the United States fail to acquire a fee simple or lesser interest in substantially all of the lands described in section 2(b) of the said act, other than improved residential property as that term is used in the act, within five years from the date of this deed;

(c) Should the United States use or permit the use or fail to prevent the use of any of the lands described in section 2(b) of the said act for any purpose or act prohibited on the lands described herein by the covenants and restrictions contained in this deed;

(d) Should the United States sell, transfer or in any way relinquish control of all or any part of the lands described in section 2(b) of the said act of Congress.

The easement and rights herein granted shall, likewise, terminate in the event it is determined by the Secretary of the Interior by means of a document published in the Federal Register that it has not been possible to accomplish the preservation objectives of the said act of October 4, 1961.

IN WITNESS WHEREOF, the parties of the first part have hereunto set their hands and seals on the day and year first above written.

_____ (Seal)

_____ (Seal)

WITNESSES:
Signed, sealed, and delivered
in the presence of

_____

_____

State of Maryland   )
) ss
County of   )

On this day the _____ day of _____ 19__,

before me personally appeared _____

_____, to me known to be the persons described in and who executed the foregoing instrument, and acknowledged that they executed the same as their free act and deed.

_____

(Notary Public)

Appendix 3

Wisconsin Scenic Easement (A-490)

(sample)

STATE OF WISCONSIN
DEPARTMENT OF NATURAL RESOURCES
Box 450
Madison, Wisconsin 53701

THIS INDENTURE made this _____ day of

_____, 19__, by and between _____

and _____, his wife,

of _____, _____ County, Wisconsin, Grantor

_____; and the State of Wisconsin (Department of Natural Resources),
Grantee.

WHEREAS, the Grantor _____, _____ the

owner _____ in fee simple of certain real estate which is in,
near to, or adjacent to a Department of Natural Resources project area

now known as _____ and located in _____
County, Wisconsin, and

WHEREAS, because the said property is so located as to be

a logical portion of the _____ the Grantee, through

its Department of Natural Resources, desires to preserve insofar as reason-

ably is possible, the natural beauty of the _____,

roadside, lake, stream area

and to prevent any unsightly developments that will tend to mar or detract from such natural beauty or to degrade the character of the project, or result in danger to travel, and to that end to exercise such reasonable controls over the lands within the restricted area described hereinafter as may be necessary to accomplish such objectives,

NOW, THEREFORE,

WITNESSETH: For and in consideration of the sum of

$_____ paid by the Grantee to the Grantor _____, receipt whereof is hereby acknowledged, and in consideration of the covenants

hereinafter contained, the Grantor _____ hereby sell, transfer, grant, and convey to the Grantee, its successors and assigns, upon acceptance by said Grantee, an easement and right in perpetuity to any and all portions of the following described real estate, which acceptance must be made by

the Grantee within _____ months from the date hereof [the description follows]:

the location of said easement being shown on Exhibit "A" attached, hereto, and made a part hereof.

(1) The price to be paid to Grantor _____ by Grantee for such easement is $_____

(2) No building or premises shall be used and no building shall hereafter be erected or structurally altered except for one or more of the following uses:

(a) [This item was left blank.]

(b) General farming, including farm buildings, except fur farms and farms operated for the disposal of garbage, rubbish, offal or sewage.

(c) Telephone, telegraph or electric lines or pipes or pipe lines or microwave radio relay structures for the purpose of transmitting messages, heat, light or power.

(d) Uses incident to any of the above permitted uses, including accessory buildings.

(e) Any use on the premises at the time of the execution of this easement. Existing commercial and industrial uses of lands and buildings may be continued, maintained and repaired, but may not be expanded nor shall any structural alteration be made.

(3) No dump of ashes, trash, sawdust or any unsightly or offensive material shall be placed upon such restricted area except as is incidental to the occupation and use of the land for normal agricultural or horticultural or _____ purposes.

(4) No sign, billboard, outdoor advertising structure or advertisement of any kind shall be erected, displayed, placed or maintained upon or within the restricted area, except one sign of not more than 8 square feet in area to advertise the sale, hire or lease of property or the sale of any products produced upon the premises.

(5) No trees or shrubs shall be removed or destroyed on the land covered by this easement, except as may be incidental to the permitted uses.

(6) The grant of this easement does in no way grant to the public the right to enter such area for any purpose.

To have and to hold the said easement hereby granted, unto the Grantee forever.

A covenant is hereby made with the State of Wisconsin that

the Grantor _____ hold _____ the premises described on the previous page included in the "restricted area" by good and perfect title; having good right and lawful authority to sell and convey the same; that the premises are free and clear from all liens and encumbrances whatsoever except as hereinafter set forth.

The Grantor _____, for themselves, their heirs, executors, administrators, grantees, successors, and assigns, further covenant that they will neither lease nor convey any other easement in any way affecting said "restricted area" without first securing the written permission of the Department of Natural Resources of Wisconsin or its successor or successors.

And _____

_____ being the

owner _____ and holder _____ of _____ certain _____

lien _____ which is _____
                                   (insert detail concerning lien)

against said premises, do _____ hereby join in and consent to said conveyance free of said lien.

WITNESS the hands and seals of the Grantor _____ and of any person joining in and consenting to this conveyance on the day and year hereinbefore written.

In presence of . . . .(SEAL)

. . . .(SEAL)

. . . .(SEAL)

. . . .(SEAL)

. . . .(SEAL)

STATE OF WISCONSIN)
) ss.
_____ COUNTY)

Personally appeared before me this _____ day of

_____, 19__, the above named _____

_____

to me known to be the persons who executed the foregoing instrument and acknowledged the same.

(NOTARY SEAL)   . . . .

Notary Public, ... County, Wisconsin

My commission expires . . . .

ACCEPTED this _____ day of _____, 19__.

STATE OF WISCONSIN
DEPARTMENT OF NATURAL RESOURCES
BY _____
(Attorney)

Appendix 4
Wisconsin Conservation Easement

The following form has been used by the Conservation Department of the State of Wisconsin in the acquisition of conservation easements for wetlands.

THIS INDENTURE made this   day of   , 19 , by and between   and   , his wife, of   County, Wisconsin, Grantor   ; and the State of Wisconsin (Conservation Commission), Grantee.

WHEREAS, the Grantor   the owner   in fee simple of certain real estate which is in, near to, or adjacent to a Wisconsin Conservation Department project area now known as   , and located in   County, Wisconsin, and

WHEREAS, the said lands contain and include wetland, marsh and water areas which the Grantee desires to obtain, protect and preserve.

NOW, THEREFORE,

WITNESSETH: For and in consideration of the sum of $........ paid by the Grantee to the Grantor   , receipt whereof is hereby acknowledged, and in consideration of the convenants hereinafter contained the Grantor hereby agree to sell, transfer, grant, and convey to the Grantee, upon acceptance by said Grantee, an easement and right in perpetuity to any and all portions of the following described real estate, including the right of access thereto, which acceptance must be made by the Grantee within   months from the date thereof:

the location of said easement being shown on Exhibit "A" attached hereto, and made a part hereof. The price to be paid to Grantor by Grantee for such easement is $..........

The Grantor   , for themselves and for their heirs, successors and assigns, covenant and agree that they will cooperate in the maintenance of the aforesaid land as wetland, including streams, springs, lakes, ponds, marshes, sloughs, swales, swamps, or potholes, now existing or hereafter occurring on the above-described tract by not draining or permitting the draining through the transfer of appurtenant water rights or otherwise, of any of said wetlands by ditching or any other means; by not filling in with earth or any other material, any low areas of said wetlands; and by not burning any areas covered with marsh vegetation.

It is understood and agreed that this indenture imposes no other obligations or restrictions upon the parties of the first part and that neither they nor their heirs, successors, assigns, lessees, or any other person or party claiming under them shall in any way be restricted from carrying on farming practices such as grazing, hay cutting, plowing, working and cropping wetlands when the same are dry of natural causes, and that they may utilize all of the subject lands in the customary manner except for the draining, filling, and burning provisions mentioned above.

To have and to hold the said easement hereby granted, unto the grantee forever.

A covenant is hereby made with the State of Wisconsin that the Grantor hold the premises described on the previous page included in the "restricted area" by good and perfect title; having good right and lawful authority to sell and convey the same; that the premises are free and clear from all liens and encumbrances whatsoever except as hereinafter set forth.

The Grantor   , for themselves, their heirs executors, administrators, grantees, successors, and assigns, further covenant and agree that they will neither lease nor convey any other easement in any way affecting said "restricted area" without first securing the written permission of the State Conservation Commission of Wisconsin or its successor or successors.

AND   being the owner and holder   of certain   lien   which is   against said premises, do hereby join in and consent to said conveyance free of said lien.

Appendix 5

Federal Government Agencies and Private Organizations Offering Assistance

FEDERAL AGENCIES

Department of Health, Education, and Welfare
330 Independence Ave. S.W., Washington, D.C. 20201
Offers a variety of assistance, including financial aid to schools, school districts, colleges, and universities in preserving and using outdoor school areas.

Department of Housing and Urban Development
Open Space Branch, 451 7th St. S.W., Washington, D.C. 20410
Provides financial assistance to communities developing broad open space programs.

Department of Agriculture
Forest Service, South Agricultural Building, 14th St. and Jefferson Drive, Washington, D.C. 20250
Provides informational materials on forests and forest management. The Soil Conservation Service provides information on soil, soil management, and wildlife. Publication: *Soil Conservation* (magazine).

Department of the Interior
National Park Service, Interior Building, Washington, D.C. 20240
Provides management aid in park development. The Bureau of Outdoor Recreation provides financial aid to states and local communities for land acquisition and development pertaining to outdoor recreation. The Bureau of Sport Fisheries and Wildlife provides guidance on wildlife refuge management. The Bureau of Land Management provides information on land management on the public lands, largely in the western states.

STATE AGENCIES

State agencies can be very useful; like federal agencies, most of them have extensive aid, educational, and publication programs, and an inquiry directed to them about available material or guidelines will usually receive prompt attention. In many cases they have staff men whose job it is to work with local groups and with landowners. The list of the names of such agencies is too long to include here. Suffice it to say that they vary from state to state; in one, for example, the principal conservation agency might be called the department of natural resources and in another, the conservation commission. However, if you write to the department of conservation and natural resources at the state capital, the letter will probably find its way to the right office. Similarly, a letter directed to the department of parks and recreation will reach the principal recreation agency, whatever its precise title. State planning agencies can be key contacts too.

Most state agencies have local offices in the principal cities, and their names, addresses, and phone numbers will be listed in the telephone directory under the main listing for the state. It is also a good idea to see if there is any listing under the particular subject you are concerned with. Look up "air" or "water" or "park" for example, and you may run across additional agencies and groups that would be of help. The telephone directory is probably the single most important tool for launching campaigns, but it is amazing how many people overlook its usefulness as a source of information.

The state university is another source of help. Increasingly, state universities are carrying on advisory and research work in environmental resource problems. Virtually every state university has an agricultural extension service, and many have services for urban problems.

PRIVATE ORGANIZATIONS

American Association of Botanical Gardens and Arboretums
Department of Horticulture, New Mexico State University, Las Cruces, New Mexico 88001
Assistance available includes planning and developing public, municipal, and institutional interests in plants. Suggestions are made regarding personnel, administration, and layout for the most effective use of an area. Publications: Quarterly Newsletter No. 61: *Planning an Arboretum*, 20 pp., $0.30.

American Association for Health, Physical Education and Recreation
1201 16th St. N.W., Washington, D.C. 20036
Dedicated to the improvement of health education, physical education, and recreation; a department of the National Education Association. The Asso-

ciation offers technical assistance through local members and state and district conferences, workshops, and clinics. Publications: *Education in and for the Outdoors*, 96 pp., $2.00, gives recommendations for development of outdoor education programs; *Outdoor Education for American Youth*, 164 pp., $1.25, a text for teaching appreciation of the outdoors; *Outdoor Education*, 32 pp., $0.75, evaluates and gives examples of activities.

American Forestry Association
919 19th St. N.W., Washington, D.C. 20006
Citizen's organization for improving management and use of forests and related resources. Publications: *American Forests* (magazine); *Trail Riders of the Wilderness*, 23 pp., free, describes pack and canoe trips into wilderness areas.

Association of Interpretive Naturalists
18454 Salem Ave., Detroit, Michigan 48219
Advances education and development of skills in interpreting the natural environment. The Association offers guidance in establishment of a nature program, securing a naturalist, and developing areas; it runs workshops on interpretive programs. Publications: pamphlets and booklets describing various nature trails and exhibits; *A Directory of Interpretive Materials*, $1.00.

American Nature Study Society
R.D. 1, Homer, New York 13077
Publication: *Nature Study* (quarterly), edited by Stanley B. Mulaik, Zoology Department, University of Utah, Salt Lake City, Utah 84112.

Conservation Education Association
Dr. Wilson S. Clark, Eastern Montana College, Billings, Montana 59101
Dedicated to the development of an education program in the public schools and in teacher-training institutions which teaches the importance of individual and organized action in making intelligent use of natural resources.

Ducks Unlimited, Inc.
National Headquarters, P.O.B. 66300, Chicago, Illinois 60666
A non-profit organization dedicated to the wise conservation of our continent's waterfowl resources, primarily through the rehabilitation, construction, and maintenance of the primary nesting and breeding areas in Canada. It maintains a full library of top-quality color and sound motion pictures. Publications: *The Ducks Unlimited Magazine* (quarterly); *The Duckological*, a monthly report on waterfowl habitat and production conditions, issued direct from the Winnipeg, Canada, offices of Ducks Unlimited.

Izaak Walton League of America
1326 Waukegan Road, Glenview, Illinois 60025
A national membership, non-profit organization devoted to the conservation and restoration of renewable natural resources. It offers land and other facilities for skeet, conservation education, trapshooting, fly and plug-casting, and camping; it also promotes lectures, films, and demonstrations of outdoor activities through local chapters. Publications: *Izaak Walton Magazine (Outdoor America)*.

National Association of Home Builders
1625 L St. N.W., Washington, D.C. 20036
A national association of local chapter home builder members, offering them advice and guidance on land use and home building. Publications: *Journal of Home Building* (monthly); *Scope* (weekly newsletter).

National Audubon Society
1130 Fifth Ave., New York, New York 10028
Publications: *Audubon Magazine* (bimonthly), $8.50 per year, $1.50 per copy; *Audubon Leader* (monthly). The Educational Services Department offers Audubon Aids in Natural Science (bird and mammal study guides, teaching bulletins on plants and animals, charts, etc.). The Audubon Wildlife film-lectures are offered to 260 American communities each year and reach about half a million people.

The Nature Center Planning Division provides guidance and counseling on community nature center development and offers professional planning assistance in nature center planning, outdoor interpretive education programming, outdoor schools, outdoor laboratories, nature parks, wildlife preserves, etc. Publications: *A Nature Center for Your Community*, 40 pp., $1.00; *Planning a Nature Center*, 88 pp., $2.00; *Manual of Outdoor Conservation Education*, 96 pp., $2.00; *Trail Planning and Layout*, 104 pp., $2.50; *Wildlife Habitat Improvement*, 96 pp., $2.50; *Manual of Outdoor Interpretation*, 104 pp., $3.00; *Guidelines to Conservation Education Action*, 132 pp., $2.50 paper, $5.00 cloth; *Directory of Environmental Education Facilities*, 40 pp., $2.50; *Nature Center News* (quarterly).

National Recreation and Park Association
1700 Pennsylvania Ave. N.W., Washington, D.C. 20006
An independent non-profit service organization dedicated to the advancement and enhancement of the park and recreation movement and the conservation of natural and human resources. It provides liaison with all levels of government on parks, recreation, and conservation, carries on research and technical studies, offers community site planning, develops standards, conducts educational information programs, and maintains a library of

pertinent books and materials. Publications: the following materials are published for members of the Association but are available for sale to non-members. *Parks and Recreation* (monthly), $5.00 per year; *Recreation and Park Yearbook*, published at five-year intervals, a statistical study of the park and recreation field, 1961–1966, $5.50; *Park Practice Program*, a series of four special publications on policies, planning, operating, and philoso-phies of the park and recreation field, $40.00 per year. The Association also publishes *Management Aids*, a series of monthly bulletins on various tech-nical topics in the park and recreation field, $2.00 per copy, $24.00 per year:

Manual for Park and Recreation Boards and Commissions, 40 pp.
Vandalism—How To Stop It, 38 pp.
Small Lake Management Manual and Survey, 44 pp.
The Loss of Park and Recreation Land, 32 pp.
Land Requirements, 36 pp.
Lake Zoning for Recreation, 30 pp.
Sources of Assistance, 45 pp.

National Wildlife Federation
1412 16th St. N.W., Washington, D.C. 20036
An association of state organizations and their affiliated local clubs, individ-ual associate members, and other private citizens, promoting conservation and wise use of natural resources. The Federation offers educational mate-rials, books, other publications, and technical advice, through a small field staff, to statewide or regional organizations. Publications: *Conservation Directory*, an annual listing of federal, state, and private organizations working in the field of natural resource use and management, $1.00; *Con-servation News* (semimonthly), free, which touches on all phases of conservation work, including outdoor recreation; *Conservation Report*, issued weekly while Congress is in session, digests resources legislation in the Congress, free; *National Wildlife*, a magazine issued six times per year as part of a $5.00 annual membership package to associate members; *Ranger Rick*, a nature magazine issued ten times per year, designed for children.

Open Space Institute
145 E. 52d St., New York, New York 10022
A non-profit, non-governmental corporation which offers assistance in urban open space planning through field programs, technical assistance, and publications.

Remington Farms
Chestertown, Maryland 20620
Program devoted to developing and demonstrating methods for managing wildlife on farmland. Literature and information on farm management for

small game and waterfowl is free on request. Publication: *Perennial Plants for Shooting Preserves*, leaflet, free, describes food and cover plants valuable to wildlife.

Sport Fishing Institute
719 13th St. N.W., Washington, D.C. 20005
A nonprofit, professionally staffed fish conservation organization, it carries out a three-point program of research in fishery biology, fish conservation education, and professional service to official conservation agencies and to its members. The Institute is dedicated to the improvement of sport fishing opportunities nationwide. Assistance available is dependent upon circumstances; it provides various kinds of advice and consultation on fish conservation matters to organizations and public groups. (It does not answer inquiries from otherwise unaffiliated individuals.) Publications: *Sport Fishing Institute Bulletin* and occasional special publications dealing with selected fish conservation subjects available free to members and at a modest cost to nonmembers.

The Nature Conservancy
1522 K St. N.W., Washington, D.C. 20005
The only national conservation organization whose sole purpose is the preservation of natural areas of outstanding scientific or aesthetic significance through their actual acquisition by purchase or gift. Staff experience and competence are available in the following areas: techniques of land acquisition; legal devices for land acquisition; state and federal resource administration; technical forestry, wildlife, and other aspects of natural science or ecology; public relations and community action; fund raising; resource planning; general business and law; Latin-American affairs. Publications: *The Nature Conservancy News* (quarterly); *Questions and Answers about The Nature Conservancy; Natural Areas*, describing how The Nature Conservancy works to preserve our heritage of wild nature; *Gifts of Land to The Nature Conservancy*, which outlines tax advantages to the individual; and *The Latin-American Desk of The Nature Conservancy*.

Urban America, Inc.
1717 Massachusetts Avenue N.W., Washington, D.C. 20036
Offers guidance in urban development, primarily housing.

Urban Institute
2100 M St. N.W., Washington, D.C.
Offers assistance on a variety of urban environmental problems.

Urban Land Institute
1200 18th St. N.W., Washington, D.C. 20036
An independent, non-profit research organization founded to promote the

better planning and development of urban areas. The Institute studies, analyzes, and reports on trends which influence the development and use of our land. Its realistic approach has made it one of America's most respected and widely quoted sources of information on urban land problems.

Wildlife Management Institute
709 Wire Building, Washington, D.C. 20005
Provides field technical assistance to private landowners on habitat improvement for wildlife. Publication: *Outdoor News Bulletin* (biweekly).

Bibliography

ABRAMS, CHARLES. "Opportunities in Taxation for Achieving Planning Purposes." *Planning 1966.* Chicago, Ill.: American Society of Planning Officials, 1966.

ASHBAUGH, BYRON L. *Trail Planning and Layout.* New York: National Audubon Society, 1965.

BATES, MARSTON. *The Forest and the Sea.* New York: Random House, 1960.

BOYLE, ROBERT H. "How To Stop the Pillage of America." *Sports Illustrated,* December 11, 1967.

CANTY, DONALD, ed. *The New City.* New York: Frederick A. Praeger, 1969.

CARTWRIGHT, DORWIN. "Achieving Change in People." *Human Relations* 4 (1951): 387–91.

CITIZENS COMMITTEE FOR THE OUTDOOR RECREATION RESOURCES REVIEW COMMISSION REPORT. *Action for Outdoor Recreation for America.* Washington, D.C.: 1001 Connecticut Ave., n.d. [Apr. 11, 1963].

CLAWSON, MARION. "A Positive Approach to Open Space Preservation." *Journal of the American Institute of Planners* 28 (1962).

CLEMENT, ROLAND C. *Man and Nature in the City.* U.S. Department of the Interior, Bureau of Sport Fisheries and Wildlife, symposium proceedings. Washington, D.C.: U.S. Government Printing Office, 1968.

CLEMENT, ROLAND C. "Open Space and the Breath of Life." Unpublished study by Dr. Ben Davidson of New York University. Available from Roland C. Clement, National Audubon Society, New York.

CONSERVATION FOUNDATION. *Implications of Rising Carbon Dioxide Content of the Atmosphere.* New York: By the Foundation, 1963.

FOSDICK, RAYMOND B. "We Must Not Be Afraid of Change." *New York Times Magazine,* April 3, 1949.

FRAZIER, KENDRICK. "Earth's Cooling Climate." *Science News* 96 (1969): 458.

GOODMAN, WILLIAM I., AND FREUND, ERIC C., eds. 1968. *Principles and Practice of Urban Planning.* Washington, D.C.: International City Managers' Association, 1968.

HALL, EDWARD T. *The Hidden Dimension.* Garden City, N.Y.: Doubleday, 1967.

HALPRIN, LAWRENCE. *Cities.* New York: Reinhold Publishing Corp., 1963.

HERFINDAHL, ORRIS C., AND KNEESE, ALLEN V. *Quality of the Environment: An Economic Approach to Some Problems in Using Land, Water, and Air.* Baltimore: Johns Hopkins Press for Resources for the Future, Inc., 1965.

KRUTILLA, JOHN V. "Conservation Reconsidered." *American Economic Review,* September 1967. Reprinted by Resources for the Future, Inc.

KUHN, ERIC. "Planning the City's Climate." *Landscape* 8 (1959): 21–23.

LINDBERGH, CHARLES A. "The Wisdom of Wildness." *Life Magazine,* December 22, 1967.

LITTLE, CHARLES E. *Challenge of the Land.* New York: Open Space Institute, 1968.

McHARG, IAN L. *Design with Nature.* Garden City, N.Y.: Natural History Press for the American Museum of Natural History, 1969.

MICHAEL, DONALD N. *The Unprepared Society.* New York: Basic Books, 1968.

MIDDLETON, JOHN T. "Air Pollution Threat to Flora and Fauna Doubles Threat to Man." *Conservation Catalyst* 2 (1967). Reprinted by U.S. Department of Health, Education, and Welfare, National Center for Air Pollution Control.

MUMFORD, LEWIS. "The Challenge of Survival." Address to the Bronx Botanical Garden seminar, Bronx, N.Y., July 10, 1968.

NATIONAL AUDUBON SOCIETY, NATURE CENTER PLANNING DIVISION. *Survey and Nature Center Plan for Reston, Virginia.* New York: By the Society, 1964.

NATIONAL AUDUBON SOCIETY, NATURE CENTER PLANNING DIVISION. *Directory of Environmental Educational Facilities.* New York: By the Society, 1969.

NATIONAL AUDUBON SOCIETY, NATURE CENTER PLANNING DIVISION. *Natural Area and Outdoor Interpretive Education Planning Services.* New York: By the Society, 1969.

OUTDOOR RECREATION RESOURCES REVIEW COMMISSION. *Outdoor Recreation for America.* Report to the President and Congress. Washington, D.C.: U.S. Government Printing Office, 1962.

PLANNING ASSOCIATES. *What Do Parks and Recreation Accomplish? Benefits to the Social Environment.* Long Island, N.Y.: Planning Associates, n.d.

PRESIDENT'S COUNCIL ON RECREATION AND NATURAL BEAUTY. *From Sea to Shining Sea.* Washington, D.C.: U.S. Government Printing Office, 1968.

PREZIOSO, SAL J. *Economic Advantages of Parklands to a Community.* Washington, D.C.: National Recreation and Park Association, 1969.

RICKERT, JOHN E. "The Present and Potential Role of State and Local Taxation in the Preservation or Development of Open Space Land in Urban Fringe Areas." Unpublished study for the Urban Land Institute, December, 1965.

SEARS, PAUL B. *The Living Landscape.* New York: Basic Books, 1966.

SHOMON, JOSEPH J. *A Nature Center for Your Community.* New York: National Audubon Society, Nature Center Planning Division, 1963.

SHOMON, JOSEPH J. "Nature Centers—One Approach to Environmental Education." *Environmental Education Journal* 1 (1969): 56–60.

SHOMON, JOSEPH J.; ASHBAUGH, BYRON L.; and TOLMAN, CON D. *Wildlife Habitat Improvement.* New York: National Audubon Society, 1966.

SIMON ENTERPRISES. *The Reston Story.* Fairfax, Va.: Simon Enterprises, 1962.

STRONG, ANN LOUISE. *Preserving Open Space.* Washington, D.C.: Urban Renewal Administration, Housing and Home Finance Agency, February, 1963.

TASK FORCE ON ENVIRONMENTAL HEALTH AND RELATED PROBLEMS. *A Strategy for a Livable Environment.* Report to the Secretary of Health, Education, and Welfare. Washington, D.C.: U.S. Government Printing Office, 1967.

UDALL, STEWART L. *The Quiet Crisis.* New York: Holt, Rinehart and Winston, 1963.

UNITED NATIONS. *Planning of Metropolitan Areas and New Towns.* New York: United Nations, 1967.

UNITED NATIONS. *Urbanization: Development Policies and Planning.* International Social Development Review, No. 1. New York: United Nations, 1968.

UNITED NATIONS. *Demographic Yearbook 1969.* New York: United Nations, 1969.

U.S. BUREAU OF THE CENSUS. *Projections of the Population of the United States by Age, Sex and Color to 1990, with Extensions of Population by Age and Sex to 2015.* Current Population Reports, Series P-25, No. 381. Washington, D.C.: U.S. Government Printing Office, 1967.

U.S. DEPARTMENT OF AGRICULTURE, FOREST SERVICE, NORTHEAST FOREST EXPERIMENT STATION. *People, Cities and Trees.* Upper Darby, Pa.: By the Department, n.d.

U.S. DEPARTMENT OF AGRICULTURE. *Major Uses of Land and Water in the United States.* Agricultural Economic Report 149. Washington, D.C.: U.S. Government Printing Office, 1964.

URBAN AMERICA, INC. *Selected New Towns in Europe.* Washington, D.C.: Urban America, 1969.

URBAN RENEWAL ADMINISTRATION, DEPARTMENT OF HOUSING AND URBAN DEVELOPMENT. *Open Space for Urban America.* Washington, D.C.: By the Administration, 1965.

WHYTE, WILLIAM H. *Cluster Development.* New York: American Conservation Association, 1964.

ZIMERING, STANLEY, AND JOHNSON, KENNETH L. "The Contaminated Air." *New York Conservationist,* October–November, 1969.

Index

169

THE JOHNS HOPKINS PRESS

Designed by Alan M. daly
Composed in Baskerville text
by Monotype Composition Company
Printed on 60 lb. Sebago Offset
by Universal Lithographers, Inc.
Bound in Columbia Riverside Linen RL 3769
by L.H. Jenkins, Inc.